GEORGIAN AND VICTORIAN CARLISLE

Life, Society and Industry

Castle with Queen Mary's Tower. Tower demolished 1834. (*W. H. Nutter*)

Georgian and Victorian Carlisle

Life, Society and Industry

Sydney Towill

Carnegie Publishing Ltd, 1996

First published by Carnegie Publishing Ltd,
18 Maynard Street, Preston PR2 2AL

ISBN 1-85936-039-4

Typsetting and origination by Carnegie Publishing, Preston
Printed and bound by Bookcraft (Bath) Ltd

Contents

Acknowledgements

I wish to acknowledge my debt to the Carlisle historians of the past two centuries who have researched in this field before me. My indebtednes is expressed in the text and bibliographies.

More directly I wish to thank present day researchers in this field who have diligently sought to answer my request for information and to supply me with prints for the copious illustrations in this book. In particular, among many contacts, I would thank Stephen White of the Cumbria County Library, Susan Dench of the Cumbria Record Office, Dawn Webster and Guy Pawle of Tullie House, Canon Weston of Carlisle Cathedral and Dennis Perrian. In addition I thank Robin Burgess for access to files of the *Cumberland News* and former *Carlisle Journal*.

Above all I have to thank my wife Dorothy for her forbearance for the long periods I have, from necessity, spent in my study researching and writing this book.

Sydney Towill
Sycamore House
Plas Newton Lane
Chester

Foreword

by The Rt Hon. The Viscount Whitelaw, KT, CH, MC

The years 1745–1875 are arguably the most significant years in the long history of Carlisle. The city had barely emerged from the medieval ages and was therefore a fortified city subject to national wars and border skirmishes, a small city without industry and with mean and primitive housing. Since then, much has developed for Carlisle. It has overcome all the difficulties of the past. It is now a very important industrial city with a very wide range of opportunities. I am sure it will be very valuable to see exactly what has evolved in Carlisle in these activities today.

I wish you every success in the plans you are putting forward in your book and wish it every success in its national endeavours today.

Chronology

1689	Tullie House built.
1698	Celia Fiennes describes city.
1717	Town Hall rebuilt.
1721	River Act to improve navigation of River Eden fails.
1724	Daniel Defoe visits city.
1724	Guliker (or Deulicher) establishes woollen manufactory.
1745	Carlisle taken, and retaken, in Jacobite rebellion.
1746	G. Blamire and Richard Ferguson linen business established.
1746	Ferguson Bros. linen manufactory at Warwick Bridge (Langthwaite Mill).
1750	R. & W. Hodgson linen manufactory.
1750s	Turnpike Trusts open up Carlisle.
1761	Scot Lamb introduce calico printing.
1762	Stage coach over Shap, but main route south via Stainmore.
1764	Barton & Wood calico printers established.
1779–1788	Dr Heysham's statistical observations – 'Carlisle life table'
1780	Porter's iron foundry Blackfriars Street.
from c. 1780	Sunday schools founded in Carlisle.
1782	Carlisle Dispensary for the poor opened.
1785	Carlisle–Manchester mail coach service.
1790	Charity school opened for girls.
c. 1790	Forsters Cotton mill at Cummersdale.
c. 1790	Demolition of Shambles and Carnaby's Folly in market place.
1795, 1812, 1817	Food riots.
1798	*Carlisle Journal* first published.
1798	Carlisle Subscription Library (initially Castle St.)
c. 1800	School of Industry opened.
1801	Forsters built print works at Cummersdale.
1804	Corporation made responsible for street lighting.
1809	Peter Dixon takes over Langthwaite mill.
1811	Lancastrian School opened.

c. 1811	Citadel replaced by Court Houses. Old English gate superseded.
c. 1811	Irish gate demolished.
1812	National School (Central School) opened.
1813	City walls demolished.
1813	*Carlisle Patriot* published.
c. 1814	Scotchgate demolished.
1814	New Eden Bridge – Priest beck becomes main channel of River Eden.
1817	Theatre built – adjacent to St Cuthberts Lane.
1819	Carlisle Gas Co. founded.
1820	Fever hospital built.
1820, 1826	Carlisle Weavers' riots.
1823	Carlisle–Port Carlisle canal opened.
1824	Joseph Ferguson Friggate works – Dyeing and finishing of cotton goods.
1824	Mechanics Institute
1826	St Patrick's school opened (Catholic sponsored).
1827	Carlisle's new police force – but of very limited strength.
1828	Joseph Ferguson extends business to Holme Head.
1829	New County Gaol built in Carlisle.
1831	Subscription library built.
c. 1834	Carr's biscuit works opens adjacent to Canal basin.
1835	Municipal Corporations Act
1835	McAlpin calico printing works opens at Cummersdale.
1835	Demolition of Guard House and replacement by Fish Market in market square.
1836	Dixon's Shaddon Mills opened, including factory school.
1838	Inauguration of Chartist movement in Carlisle.
1839	Newcastle and Carlisle Railway completed.
1840	Athenaeum built.
1840	Walsham Report on dwellings of labouring classes.
1841	Cumberland Infirmary completed.
1842	Chadwick's report on sanitation
1842	Council appoint Mendicant Society to enquire into state of poor.
1843	Two new National Schools built, Trinity in Caldewgate and Christ Church in Botchergate.
1845	Dr Reid Report on state of large towns.
1845	Carlisle & Maryport Railway opened.
1846	Lancaster & Carlisle Railway completse link to London.
1846	Carlisle Waterworks Co. formed.

1848	Carlisle–Glasgow Railway opened.
1847–8	Citadel Station built. Enlarged in 1873–6.
1850	Rawlinson Report on health of Carlisle.
1850	Nelson Bridge opens up Caldew Industrial area to city.
c. 1850	Ragged school opened.
1852	Water carriage sewage dispersal system introduced into Carlisle.
1854	Carlisle–Port Carlisle canal converted to railway.
1856	Carlisle–Silloth Railway opened.
1857	Carlisle police force augmented.
1857	Cowen Sheldon works, St Nicholas Street opens.
1859	Pratchett's Denton Iron Works.
1859	New dock opened at Silloth.
1860	Silloth a thriving holiday resort.
1865	Corporation takes over water supply.
1868	Hudson Scott new factory, James Street.
1869	Cowans Sheldon, St Nicholas works.
1870	Education Act Board Schools
c. 1870	Hudson Scott works at James Street opens.
1872	Isaac Teasdale factory established.
1872	Dixon's declared bunkrupt.
1874	John Laing's builders, formed.
1874	Carlisle's first Medical Officer of Health appointed.
1876	Carlisle–Settle railway.
1880	William Coulthard die-casting plant founded.
1882	Buck's Atlas Works.
1883	Dixon's cease to trade.
1883	Carlisle Grammar School moves to Spring Gardens Lane.
1887	Carr's flour mill at Silloth erected.
1898	Water Act to obtian water from Geltdale Valley.
1899	Electric Light and Power Station opens at James Street.
1900	Electric trams.
1900	Morton Sundour established.
1902	Education Act: Transfer of functions of School Boards to County and Borough Councils. Provision for secondary and technical schools.

The disadvantage of men not knowing the past is that they do not know the present. History is a hill or high point of vantage, from which alone men see the town in which they live, or the age in which they are living. Without some contrast or comparison, without some shifting of the point of view, we should see nothing whatever of our social surroundings. We should take them for granted, as the only possible social surroundings.

G. K. Chesterton

Introduction

The years 1745–1875 are arguably the most significant in the long history of Carlisle. At the beginning of the period the city had barely emerged from the medieval ages. A fortified city subject to national wars and border skirmishes; a small city without industry and with mean and primitive housing; a self-contained city cut off from the rest of England by its geographical position except for occasional visits by intrepid travellers and pack-horse trains. At the end of the period Carlisle was a thriving industrial city with an important national and international trade. A city linked by turnpike roads and canal to the rest of the country, and finally by a railway system which would change the pattern of Carlisle's industry and open up the city for trade and cultural exchange. By 1875 Carlisle was a significant city in economic terms, with a population that had increased eightfold during the period of 130 years.

Superficially the history of Carlisle can be described and explained in economic terms; the development of the transport system by road and canal, a vigorous cotton industry stimulated by ingenious inventions, followed by the diversification of trade with the coming of the railways. A period of rapidly growing population with a great increase in material wealth. But a summing up is a gross simplification of the events of 130 years, which would be barely recognisable by contemporaries, a treatment of Carlisle and its citizens as an homogeneous entity marching steadily and inexorably to a brighter and more prosperous future. Such a description is an interpretive pattern imposed upon very diverse events by a later generation with the advantage of hindsight. But to contemporary witnesses the line of development was not unambiguously laid out. Progress in this context is a selective and partial term, indeed to a large body of the citizens the course of events appeared as a social and economic regression. The citizens of Carlisle were not a homogeneous unit, for much of the time they were a conglomeration of diverse groups with conflicting sectional interests and widely different material fortune.

Chesterton's topographical analogy of the hill or high vantage point, from which to see the town in which one lives, and his shifting point of view, must be transferred to the temporal and heterogeneous series of events implicit in the word history. To shift our view point and to view the history of Carlisle through the eyes of contemporaries is to add a variety and a richness to the city's history and to make intelligible events which to us would otherwise appear inexplicable or obtuse.

Pride of place in this history must be given to a new breed of citizen, the industrial entrepreneurs, men of vigour, imagination and courage who seized the opportunity to exploit the new machines for the spinning of cotton. They built up vast industrial enterprises to make their fortunes, and at the same time they made a cheap and superior article for the benefit of all. With the limited resources at their disposal their achievement was staggering. Complementing Carlisle's industry was the development of transport systems, successively turn-pike roads, canal and railways, that were to integrate Carlisle into the national economy. Without an efficient transport system for the carriage of bulk goods Carlisle's large scale industry would not have been possible.

But economic development in Carlisle was not a neat orderly process, but one of conflicting interests. For the more fortunate there was a great increase in material well-being, a supply of cheap domestic goods never before experi-enced, and a growth of cultural awareness due to the greatly expanded horizon arising from the revolutionary growth in transport. Yet the very concept of progress could be questioned by many citizens. The fate of that most depressed sector of the community, the domestic hand-loom weaver for instance, grew steadily worse as the factory system expanded. As he tried to compete, at a hopeless disadvantage, with the factory machine, his earnings barely reached subsistence level. With poverty went overcrowding, insanitary conditions and disease resulting from an exponential growth at Carlisle of 20% or 30% per decade in the first half of the 19th century and the absence of civic planning and intervention before the belated social investigations of the 1840s. An examination of contemporary newspapers, histories and transcripts of Parlia-mentary debates tells us a great deal of the social attitudes in a deeply divided society. There are blunt and uninhibited references to the lower orders, and this was more than a mere turn of phrase, it was more a recognition of a society on two levels. Later chapters will record actions of our forebears that today seem monstrous. The harshness of the factory system, the exploitation of children, the horrendous punishments enacted for seemingly minor offences against property, the acceptance of abject poverty amongst a large section of the population, and the fatalistic toleration of squalor and disease. The window through which the twentieth-century reader views past events presents an inexplicable picture, but rather than think that human nature has changed after the eighteenth/nineteenth centuries it will be more rewarding to look at the cultural ambience of this earlier period and judge our ancestors' actions on this context. We can do this by studying contemporary documents and the work of contemporary authors. Their reports on factual events, and above all their conceptual outlook and opinions, will give a more understandable, if not more acceptable, picture of a past epoch. The works of the Archdeacon Paley of Carlisle on law and order; The Commissioners' reports on the state of large towns which give a description of the squalor of urban living; the reports of travellers; the editorial comments of newspapers, and the reports on Parliamentary committees will open a window on to the very different world of the 18th and 19th centuries.

The fact that Carlisle is a microcosm of the nation as a whole where legislative action is concerned, will not be lost sight of. The problems of law and order, the regulation of labour in factories, and the extension of national and local government in Carlisle, cannot be divorced from legislation enacted on the national scene. This legislation will be referred to where necessary in text and appendices.

Present-day Carlisle has evolved from the eighteenth-century city. The shape of modern central Carlisle is essentially the same as it was in the eighteenth century as will be evident from the study of the maps included this book, but one regrets that the inner ring road should have so decisively separated town from castles, even if one admits that they were separated for defensive reasons in the medieval city.

But while the large scale topography remains almost identical, the change in appearance is profound. Compare the handsome and dignified intramural city of today with the eighteenth-century city described by Hutchinson.

Carlisle at the beginning of the present [eighteenth] century exhibited no marks of modern convenience and elegance. The buildings mostly of wood, clay and laths bespoke of the poverty and bad taste of the inhabitants . . . the streets, though spacious were paved with large stones and the centre part, or causeway, rose to a considerable height. The fronts from the houses were paved in the same manner, the consequences of which were that the kennels or gutters were deep trenches, and stone bridges were placed in many different parts, for the convenience of passing from one side of the street to the other. These gullies were the reservoir of all kinds of filth where, when a sudden heavy rain happened, by stopping the conduit of the bridges, inundated the streets so as to render them impassable on foot . . . the houses did not exceed the height of one storey and were chiefly covered with thatch.[2]

Compare also Hutchinson's description of the primitive economy of Carlisle in the mid-eighteenth century.

Little more than half a century ago . . . their trade consisted in that of a good weekly market, two annual fairs, and two extraordinary well attended statutes for hiring servants . . . the business for the whole year was settled at these meetings [the fairs], as in many places the intercourse between town and town, or man and man, was not yet carried on by way of post carriers and other public conveyances . . . the necessaries of life were uncommonly cheap and the chief part of their wearing apparel was of their own spinning . . . pride and luxury in eating, drinking, furniture and dress had not yet made their entrance within the city walls.[3]

It is from this mean and backward base that modern Carlisle has evolved. The dominant influence in this transformation was the industrial revolution of the eighteenth and nineteenth centuries which generated wealth never previously imagined. By the end of the nineteenth century Carlisle had a diversified and better balanced industrial base which supported a greatly extended service sector, an augmented, but not universal, level of prosperity, and fundamentally a more humane and healthy society.

The date 1875 has been chosen arbitrarily as the end of the industrial revolution in Carlisle but a postscript extends, in lesser detail, Carlisle's industrial history through the twentieth century. Traumatic changes occurred in this period in the demise of many of the great Carlisle textile firms and the end, or change in ownership, of other firms. In the changed industrial environment of today it is opportune to pause and remember our roots.

NOTES

1. G. K. Chesterton, *All I Survey* (1933)
2. W. Hutchinson, *History of the County of Cumberland*, vol. 2 (1794)
3. Ibid.

CHAPTER I

Early Transport Development

Adam Smith, the eighteenth-century economist, wrote of the great dis-advantage suffered by inland areas of the country which possessed no good access to the sea or navigable rivers. He said

> The inland parts of the country can for a long time have no other market for the greater part of their goods but the country which lies round about them and separates them from the sea coast and the great navigable rivers. The extent of their market, must for a long time be in proportion to the riches and populousness of that country, and consequently their improvement must always be in posterior to the improvement of that country.[1]

A legacy of political instability, and the inaccessibility of Carlisle in a region cut off by mountains traversed only by rudimentary tracks had long presented insurmountable problems to external trade. A poor and backward countryside gave few compensating opportunities for a substantial local trade. And yet from the mid eighteenth century a series of transport innovations provided the stimulus that permitted the growth of a thriving textile industry, an explosive rise in population and a great increase in material wealth. The aim of this chapter will be to trace the development of the transport systems that trans-formed Carlisle from an isolated community to a thriving industrial city.

The poverty of Carlisle and the surrounding countryside, the absence of trade, and the deplorable condition of the roads in the mid eighteenth century had been noted by local historians. Ferguson reported 'the roads in Cumberland, except fro the military road, were little better than organised ruts.' Mannix and Whellan confirmed their inadequacy 'Until the middle of the eighteenth century the roads in Cumberland and the adjoining counties consisted of narrow lanes fitted only for the transit of pack horses.'[2]

An enquiry must be directed to the initiatives, that enabled Carlisle to be transformed from a poor city, with no outside trade, in 1750, to one of the four great textile manufacturing centres in Britain by the early decades of the nineteenth century.[3]

At a risk of over-simplification three distinct periods will be singled out when efforts were made to improve the transport facilities in Cumberland, and in Carlisle in particular. These initiatives were:

1. Three local entrepreneurs set out to meet the need for cheap riverborne transport for high bulk commodities such as fuel; agricultural requirements

for the land such as lime and manure; and agricultural produce, in particular grain.

2 The promotion of Turnpike Trusts *c.* 1750 by the great landowners to permit the commercial exploitation of their estates. The Carlisle-Newcastle Turnpike Trust will be treated as a special case as the motivation came from the military.

3. The first tentative proposals were made to link Carlisle to the sea by a waterway *c.* 1790, to facilitate the movement of raw materials into the city and to open up the market for the products of industry. This scheme, strongly supported by leading Carlisle industrialists, did not come to fruition until 1823.

The first notable attempt in the eighteenth century to improve communications to Carlisle was to restore an earlier limited trade by sea from collieries in the Maryport area via the Solway and the River Eden, the then overland to Carlisle, which had been rendered uneconomic by the imposition of coastal duties. The initiative came, not from the great land owners and gentry, the men of substantial financial resources, but from three Carlisle citizens Thomas Pattinson, John Hicks and Henry Orme who sought an Act of 1721 to waive coastal duties between Ellen Foot (Maryport) and Bank End, on the River Eden, to build wharfes, cranes and warehouses, and to dredge the Eden as necessary. The preamble to the Act stated:

> . . . the river is very shallow and except at times of high water, there was a great want of fuel and other necessities . . . several vast tracts of ground lying waste and uncultivated for want of water carriage of coals, lime and other manure for that purpose, renders it impossible for the said inhabitants to burn lime sufficient to lay on and improve the same, the improvement whereof would employ, relieve and be very advantageous to the poor who at present are a very great burthen to the parishes near and adjoining to the said river.[4]

The River Act passed in 1721 gave powers, for thirty-one years, to levy tolls of 8*d.* a ton on coal, lime and limestone, and 1*s.* 4*d.* on cinders, and it remitted the coastal duties. The powers given were restricted, the channel could be cleared and deepened, but no authority was given to straighten the river, to make cuts or to raise the water level. But the financial climate at the time, in the aftermath of the South Sea Bubble, was not propitious and no further action was taken.

The second period of transport innovations for Cumberland was initiated by the formation of Turnpike Trusts in the 1750s which led to a higher order of land transportation that permitted the build up of a thriving textile industry in Carlisle and which opened up the county both for the businessmen, and for the man of means and leisure. The transformation that was to occur can be better appreciated in the light of transport inadequacy of the early eighteenth century. How harrowing it then was for the traveller can be cleaned from Lord Harley's papers that reveal the inordinate slowness of long distance travel for both passengers and commerce.

Lord Harley's account of his journey from Hexham to Carlisle on 31 May 1725 was not an incentive for people to travel.

> From Hexham to the Long Byers are computed 17 miles and we are coming it eight hours twenty minutes, a way which no coaches hardly ever know to pass but those of the Judges who are necessitated to go through it once a year, and where persons of a less share of wisdom than those learned gentlemen would hardly travel over twice without some urgent occasion.[5]

Lord Harley proceeded south from Carlisle to Penrith with less complaint and made marginally better time. 'This is computed 16 miles and we came it in 5 hours and twenty five minutes.' A modest time even for a walker! Carlisle not surprisingly was a late starter in road carrier and coach services, but there is a reference to a coach from Carlisle to London which completed the journey in nine days in 1734.[6] Pack horse trains would have provided the normal form of transport at this time, but the journey time of 12–18 days from Carlisle to London[7] was exceedingly slow.

The Turnpike Acts largely removed the burden of trunk roads from the parishes to bodies authorised to charge tolls, which provided an equitable means of financing road improvements, chargeable to the people who used the roads. The first turnpike road to be constructed from Carlisle, however, was primarily for military, not commercial, purposes. General Wade's relief column from Newcastle failed to relieve Carlisle during the Jacobite invasion of 1745 because of appalling road conditions.[8] Indeed in three days the relief force had reached no further than Hexham before it came to a full stop.

The 1751 Act was '. . . for laying out, making and keeping in repair, a road proper for the passage of troops and carriages from the City of Carlisle to the Town of Newcastle upon Tyne.' The preamble states specifically 'that the road cannot be laid out, or the charge for making the same be defrayed, otherwise than at the expense of the public and by the authority of Parliament, . . .' but . . . it is apprehended that such public roads when finished may be supported and kept in repair by proper tolls and duties.'[9] A sum of £3,000 was voted for the work, two-thirds going to the Northumberland sector and one-third to Cumberland. Thereafter further grants were obtained by petitioning Parliament each year. By the time the road had been completed in 1758 £16,500 and £7,500 had been spent on the Northumberland and Cumberland sectors respectively.[10, 11]

The lack of technical expertise, and the use of inexperienced surveyors was to lead to disappointing results on the early roads, in particular on the military road. The nineteenth century writer, Cadwallader Bates, reported that the Military Road was '. . . the worst engineered road in the country. Indeed within living memory parts of the central sector of the causeway had deteriorated to a pair of ruts with grass growing between them.'[12] More unfortunate for posterity the route of Hadrian's Wall in Northumberland had excellent attributes to recommend it to the road builders. It ran in a straight line, it formed an ancient division between estates and this could be built upon without violating boundaries, and it provided a convenient quarry.

The scale of tolls laid down by Parliament was related to size of conveyance, only indirectly to weight. Thus 2s. was charged for a coach, or carriage with six or more horses, and pro rata down to a pair of horses. The Act envisaged that pack-horses would still be used, and charged 2d. for a horse or beast of burden, while drovers of cattle and sheep were charged 4d. and 2s. respectively for the Cumberland section of the road. Exemptions for tolls were granted to the military, churchgoers and farmers on local journeys. Additionally, land-owners and farming interests were looked after by toll exemptions for carting manure, limestone, or coal for burning limestone into lime and to exploit mineral resources.

The spate of Turnpike Acts passed in 1755 that opened up Carlisle to London, Lancashire, Yorkshire and West Cumberland were strictly on a commercial basis without Government grants. This was something new in the early capitalist society, a long term project for mutual benefit but with little hope of an early return on capital, and on a scale and complexity that required the pooling of capital of many people. It is not plausible to think of the Cumbrian landowners setting out to be commercial entrepreneurs, more probably they subscribed to the Trusts because of potential benefits to their own estates, to transport their agricultural products and mineral assets and to bring in their agricultural raw materials, e.g. lime and manure. But there was a price to be paid for these new facilities and not all were happy to pay it. Mannix and Whellan wrote, 'When local acts were obtained for their improvement, the exaction of tolls gave rise to much popular fury, the people then not clearly seeing that the advantages obtained by good roads greatly counter-balanced the amount of tolls levied for their formation and repair'.[13]

The new Acts were the Carlisle–Penrith–Eamont Bridge Turnpike[14] and the route was extended into Yorkshire to join the Great North Road by the Borough–Eamont Bridge Turnpike over Stainmore,[15] and over Shap into Lancashire by the Hyning Syke–Kirby in Kendal–Eamont Bridge Turnpike[16] and into mid-Yorkshire by the Keighley–Kirby in Kendal Turnpike.[17] Carlisle was also connected to West Cumberland by the Carlisle–Workington Turn-pike.[18] Before the Turnpike Acts of the 1750s, Carlisle was isolated economically with minimal industry apart from 2 small woollen and linen works of only local importance. The roads were deplorably maintained with reluctance by the parishes through which they passes, relying on untrained and unpaid parish surveyors and statute labour. With the Turnpike Acts Parliament authorised groups of investors to erect gates on major roads and to charge toll for passage. The higher standard of road which resulted permitted long distance coach and carrier services to operate. This had a dramatic effect on hitherto isolated Carlisle.

Appendix No. 3 and the Chronology record a proliferation of spinning factories and print fields, established between 1750 and the opening of the Carlisle Canal in 1823. Major enterprises include Forster's Cotton Mill at Cummersdale, and Dixon's at Langthwaite. Encouragingly, the road system was adequate to supply the Carlisle Gas Company (1819) and Porter's Iron Foundry (1780) with coal.

The inauguration of turnpike roads soon produced great changes in the pattern of inland transport from Carlisle. Mannix and Whellan wrote 'the halt or hampers of the pack horses gave place to carts', post-chaises were introduced in 1754 and carrier waggons in 1757.[19] In 1762 a stage coach was running over Shap for the first time, but the journey was still very difficult and the road over Stainmore was still the main route from Cumbria to London in the eighteenth century.[20]

The pack horse trains were not immediately rendered obsolete. Williams has calculated that 230 pack horses were regularly entering and leaving Kendal each week during the 1770s, but they were exceedingly slow and the journey from Kendal to London usually took 18 days.[21] Carlisle was to enjoy a boom in long distance travel with the inauguration of coaches, mail and carrier services. There is a wealth of information in the columns of the *Cumberland Pacquet*. For instance the 'Princess Royal' a new and elegant coach, made its inaugural run between Carlisle and London in March 1788, with a journey time of two and a half days. The itinerary sheds a great deal of light on the harsh life of the eighteenth century.

A 6.00a. m. start from Carlisle with a stay at Penrith for breakfast, then to Greta Bridge where dinner was available. Then to Borough Bridge for supper. Next day, in the absence of severe hills, a journey of 140 miles, with meal breaks at Doncaster, Grantham and Huntington.

The following day a morning ride to London. The fare was £3 15s. od. for inside passengers and half price for outside. Passenger baggage was limited to 14lbs. The return coaches to Carlisle connected with the Glasgow and Edinburgh diligences for an evening start. At average speeds of 10 m.p.h. the journeys were long and uncomfortable, especially for the coachmen and outside passengers. At this time many people did not survive what we term middle age.

In a few years a mail service was introduced, superseding the post boys, and euphemism for old men, poorly mounted, who took their time on the journey. The first mail service, inspired by John Palmer, a Bristol businessman, started between Bristol and London on 2 August 1784, with the journey completed in less than a quarter of the time taken by the post boys.[22] When Palmer was appointed Comptroller General in 1785, a rapid development of mail service ensued, and the Carlisle–Manchester mail coach service was inaugurated the same year. Posting stages were established on all coach routes, for the changing of horses after about 14 miles, and the changing of crews after 70 miles. The large scale organisation set up to run the co-ordinated services necessitated the stabling of 80 coach horses at Carlisle.

Perhaps it is not fanciful to detect in the scheduling of the mail coaches a growing response to the requirements of the merchant and businessman, for by 1829 it was possible to receive a letter from London, Manchester and Liverpool to connect to the mail service to Glasgow and Edinburgh in each direction without delay. Improved surfaces of turnpike roads and improvements in coach construction enabled a considerable speeding up with close scheduling of services throughout all season of the year. In the 1830s the London journey was down to two days and eventually down to the extraordinary time of 32 hours.[23]

The improvement in the mail service was not confined to speed and reliability in transit, the reduction in cost within another 2 decades was to be even more dramatic. At this time the cost of posting a letter was related to the distance carried, and was paid by the recipient. Post Office Archives disclose that, in 1823, a letter from Carlisle to London cost 13d. (the old style penny, $\frac{1}{240}$ of a pound), to Manchester, 10d. and to Newcastle 7d. Yet even at this time there was a hint of future developments with a penny post scheme operating in the districts of Manchester, Newcastle (Staffs), and Bristol. In 1840 Rowland Hill revolutionised the postal service with the introduction of a penny post, prepaid, for any distance throughout the United Kingdom. The great benefit to commerce and to the individual was particularly felt in geographically remote Carlisle.

A parallel development of carrier services took place. Messrs Handley '. . . advised the public of expeditious waggons in 7 days from Carlisle to London, twice a week, by way of York'.[24] The service was an integrated one with inter-connecting services from Leeds to all parts of the south. The waggon and cart facilities at this time were expanding with a weekly service of two waggons to London, six waggons to Newcastle, two waggons to Kendal, five carts to Edinburgh, four carts to Glasgow, and four carts to Whitehaven.[25] Hutchinson reminds us that Carlisle was the great thorough-fare between England and Scotland and in this branch of commerce there were about 200 horses employed.[26] The opening up of road transport gave rise to considerable material and social changes and opened up new horizons for the citizens of Carlisle. Bailey and Culley wrote '. . . the turnpike roads have brought the manners of the capital to the extremity of the Kingdom. The simplicity of ancient times has gone. Finer clothes, better dwellings and more expensive viands are now sought by all,'[27] while Nicholson and Burn noted '. . . that few people now make their own clothes. In their articles of clothes they have departed of late years from their ancient simplicity.[28]

The growing momentum towards an industrial society necessitated a better method of road construction than could be provided by the traditional system of road maintenance by unpaid and untrained local surveyors or even by Turnpike Trusts. A great improvement in road construction in the early nineteenth century was due to Thomas Telford, the eminent constructor of roads, bridges and canals. As a canal engineer he was aware of the importance of gradients and he aimed to reduce road gradients to the order of 1:40, greatly to the advantage of horse-drawn traffic. He provided strong foundations and adequate cambers on the roads and side ditches to drain away water, and built bridges to avoid costly detours. He built the Carlisle–Glasgow (1815) and the Carlisle–Port Patrick roads with strong Government support for political reasons. The Act of Union of 1800 joined Ireland to the United Kingdom and with 100 Irish MPs at Westminster, there was adequate motivation to fund the London–Holyhead and Carlisle–Port Patrick roads to ensure good communication to Dublin and Northern Ireland. Similarly in Scotland in the early

Thomas Telford (1757–1834), first President of the Institution of Civil Engineers, 1818. Pre-eminent constructor of roads, bridges, aqueducts and harbours in Britain. Consultant for Carlisle Canal and constructor of North road from Carlisle and Metal Bridge. (Photograph courtesy of the Institution of Civil Engineers)

Telford's Metal Bridge over the River Esk on the Great North Road (A7) from Carlisle was one of the earliest iron bridges in the country. Unequal spans give it an undulating appearance. (*Tullie House*)

A view of the Metal Bridge from the road. (*Tullie House*)

nineteenth century, Telford was building a network of roads in the Highlands, and it was good sense to provide a first class road from Carlisle to Glasgow.

The result of considerable logistical achievement of the road builders in opening up Carlisle to the country as a whole must not be under-estimated. An early indication of the commercial significance was the early introduction of a calico printing business to Carlisle by the Newcastle firm of Scot Lamb in 1761, a few years after the completion of the Newcastle and Carlisle turnpike. By the beginning of the nineteenth century, Carlisle had a thriving cotton industry. But the turnpikes had a wider significance than the building up of industry and the transactions of commerce, they opened up the country to the

Lamp bracket and name plate from the Metal Bridge, now in the grounds of Tullie House. (*Tullie House*)

traveller intent on pleasure. Wordsworth comments in 1805 on visitors to the Lake District: 'for travellers after pleasure are becoming not less active, and more numerous, than those who formerly left their houses for purposes of gain.'[29] The trickle became a flood when the Kendal-Windermere railway was opened in 1847.

By the beginning of the nineteenth century the need for bulk transport to and from Carlisle was becoming urgent if Carlisle was to realise its full industrial potential. While a thriving textile industry had been built up supported by land carriage of goods, a larger scale industry required a cheaper transport system for the import of raw materials and the export of finished goods to national and international markets. Overland conveyance of coal for industrial use was expensive and large scale imports of lime were required to improve agricultural land. Meanwhile the population of the city had risen dramatically from 4,000 in 1750 to 9,600 in 1790. The stage was now set for the third era of transport innovation.

Carlisle Canal

The first recorded plea for a canal to link Carlisle to the sea was made in the Universal British Directory of 1790 which recognised a flourishing but limited Carlisle economy.

> The increase of population is owing to the advance in trade and manufacturers, at present flourishing and progressive. Carlisle, from it central situation, is well adjusted for the extension of trade, and may be the exertion of a liberal and public spirit, vie with the first manufacturing towns in the Kingdom. A canal from the Western sea to Carlisle would facilitate the progress of trade, increase the wealth of the rich, and make living more comfortable to the poor.[30]

There was by this time a wide recognition that water born transport, which had a carrying capacity of a higher order of magnitude to road transport, was necessary if Carlisle was to maintain its position as an industrial town. Adam Smith had recently quantified this advantage. He considered the logistics for the transportation of 200 tons of goods from London to Edinburgh by land and by sea. The cheapest road carriage would require 50 great waggons, 100 men and 400 horses. The same load could be transported in approximately the same time in a ship of 200 tons with a crew of six or eight men.[3132]

Three of the remarkable polymaths of the late eighteenth and early nineteenth centuries who played dominant roles in the development of industrial Britain, viz. William Chapman,[33] Thomas Harrison[34] and Thomas Telford[35] were now to take the stage in putting forward plans for the construction of a canal from Carlisle to the sea, to permit the further expansion of the thriving industry of the city and to enable it to become a great trading centre, the 'Emporium of north west England.' They recognised the limitations of road and transport and foresaw the need for direct access to British and Continental markets, and especially to the markets, and cotton supplies, of the West Indies and North America.

In 1794 the first scheme was submitted, 'a canal across the narrow waist of Britain between Newcastle and Carlisle and Maryport' by Chapman. Chapman asserted

> The facility of communications with both seas and various intermediate parts of the Kingdom may probably cause new manufacturers to arrive at the already flourishing town of Carlisle.[36]

The sea to sea scheme was however more enthusiastically supported by Newcastle men than by Carlisle men who looked westward to a coastal traffic with Liverpool, Ireland and West coast Scottish ports. The next attempt was in 1807 when, after a public meeting, a committee was formed in Carlisle to promote a canal to the sea to provide the city with a better coal supply and Chapman was asked to report. Chapman gave his preference for Maryport with its existing harbour and coal supplies as a terminus, but thought if an estimated cost of £90,000 to £100,000 was too great a terminus east of Bowness would be practicable. A canal to take

William Chapman, 1748–1832, Constructor of Carlisle Canal and canals in Ireland and docks in England and Scotland. (*Science Museum*)

45 ton craft capable of making the short coastal voyage to Maryport would cost about £40,000, but if this could be enlarged to take 90 ton sea going vessels, at an extra cost of £55,000 to £60,000, these could trade to all parts of the Irish Sea, and through the Forth–Clyde canal to reach north sea ports.[37]

Thomas Harrison now entered upon the scene with a more grandiose proposal. He asserted that

> that market for cotton goods has already a reputation next to that of Manchester . . . [but] a large manufacturing town should feel the heavy disadvantage of inland carriage which at all times contracts the scale of manufactured goods and mercantile commodities.[38]

Carlisle would have every advantage if it were not subject to the expense and inconvenience of land carriage in circulating her manufactured goods through a widely extended country. But the answer was not a canal that would allow only the passage of small coastal vessels with a necessary transhipment at the nearest port, such a scheme would have little advantage over land carriage to that port. Harrison therefore proposed a canal capable of taking ships of 400–500 tons which would be able to trade to America and the West Indies without transhipment. The merchants of Scotland would come to Carlisle for what they draw from Liverpool. He held out the prospect that

Crown & Mitre coffee house and coaching inn, demolished c. 1904 for the site of
the Crown & Mitre Hotel. Glovers Row is on the left. Note the overhead
electricity distribution cables and support for tramcar supply cables.
(*Tullie House, photograph by D. I. Wilson*)

> though its manufactories have greatly increased of late years, an open com-
> munication with the sea would call into existence all that life and energy
> which an industrious county would raise up, as soon as commerce could
> spread its wings . . . Different kinds of manufactories are constantly estab-
> lishing at Carlisle and the neighbouring towns; and industry promotes the
> greater multiplication of them.

The Committee, no doubt apprehensive about the magnitude of the undertaking,
and perhaps perplexed by the number of alternative proposals, decided to consult
the country's leading engineer Thomas Telford the following year. Telford
agreed with the Bowness site for a port and he did not envisage any alternative
to a road or canal with an extension to Newcastle ultimately. But again he put
forward alternatives to the Committee for the size, and cost, of the canal varying
from locks sizes of 20ft wide to take coasting vessels; locks 14ft 9ins wide similar
to the successful Bridgewater Canal, to locks 7ft wide for narrow boats. The
later two curtailed schemes would, however, involve transhipment.[39] Again the
Committee deferred a decision with Carlisle still relying upon the River Eden
for bulk transport. It is recorded that at the time six trading vessels were operating
from Liverpool and sailing up the River Eden to Sandsfield. The average tonnage
was 35 per boat.[40] A major problem of Sandsfield as a port, however, was the
inability of sailing boats to reach there in face of an easterly wind, and the
necessary 7–8 mile load haul to Carlisle.

The Canal Basin, prints by J. W. Carmichael, 1835.
Top: note the steam locomotive with railway tracks (?) on the right of the picture.
Bottom: the basin is seen surprisingly high above the River Caldew, with a pano-
ramic view of the city, with the Castle, Cathedral and Citadel prominent. Sailing
ships were used for the short and sheltered sea voyages from Port Caslisle to Maryport, where cargo would be transferred to ocean-going ships. (*Tullie House*)

In 1818 Chapman again submitted a report.[41] He recommended a canal from Fisher's Cross to Carlisle with, in the future, the addition of a smaller canal to Newcastle. The report envisaged that the canal from Carlisle to the Solway could take the small coasters which would be capable of the short, and sheltered, coastal voyage from Fisher's Cross to Maryport, or nearby ports, from where cargoes could be transhipped to ocean going ships. Chapman commented:

> Looking to Carlisle as an emporium to the adjacent country, and the seat of manufacturers, nothing can be equivalent to its want but a direct conveyance to and from all the adjacent ports from which the materials of its manufacture, and those conducive to its process, can be obtained. Amongst these, coals are not the least important . . .[42]

His report was accepted. It was significant that the subscriptions from the Carlisle industrialists now matched those from the great landowners, an indication not only of a substantial cotton industry in Carlisle before the advent of the canal, and also a recognition that bulk transport by waterways was required if the industry was to continue to grow and prosper.[43] Chapman's estimate of the annual tonnage for shipment by canal is given in Appendix No. 3 of his report. While heavy materials, e.g. fuel, lime and stone, formed the major part of the cargo by weight the extent of the estimated transport of high value, low weight goods, e.g. cotton wool and yarn, and manufactured goods for export, were a measure of the value of the cotton industry at this time.[44]

The act of 1819 entitled 'An Act for making and maintaining a navigable canal from, or from near, the City of Carlisle to the Solway Firth, at or near Fisher's Cross in the parish of Bowness in the County of Cumberland'[45] authorised a capital of £80,000 in £50 shares and £40,000 more if necessary. The location Fisher's Cross referred to was the future Port Carlisle.[46] The Carlisle Canal Company was formed to build and operate the canal, the stated aim of which was to form a communication between the sea and the City of Carlisle shorter and safer than the navigation the Solway Firth and the River Eden afforded, and to facilitate the conveyance of lime, coal and general merchandise to and from the said city.

The canal was built and was opened in 1823. As constructed it was 11¾ miles long, 54ft wide at surface and 8ft 6in deep with locks 18ft 3in wide and 78ft long. A wooden jetty was built into the Solway at Port Carlisle and the basin approached through an entrance lock. In all there were eight additional locks, before reaching the Carlisle basin, which measured 450ft by 120ft. The total rise from the sea being 70ft. The route was favourable, no over-bridge being necessary, enabling the canal to be used by coastal craft of less than 100 tons burden. The canal was supplied with water from the Rivers Eden and Caldew, and from a reservoir on the south side of the canal in the parishes of Grinsdale and Kirkandrews-upon-Eden.

Wednesday, 12 March 1823, was a momentous date in the development of modern Carlisle. The opening of the canal transformed a rather remote city dependent for its commercial links on the limited capacity of the turnpike roads, or a difficult connection to the sea via the River Eden, to a city with a cheap and reliable bulk transport system which would enable it to be integrated into the national economic system. The significance of the occasion was not lost on Carlisle citizens. The opening ceremony was a great occasion in the history of the city.

The *Carlisle Journal* reported:[47]

. . . the opening proved more attractive in drawing together an immense concourse of spectators than any public transaction that had ever occurred (in Carlisle) . . . Upon a moderate calculation there could not be less than 18 or 20 thousand persons present upon that memorable occasion, having poured out the greater part of their inhabitants to witness the most novel and interesting spectacle . . . every yard of ground for a considerable distance round the Basin was densely covered with men, women and children in their holiday clothes.[48]

The city, as distinct from the Canal Basin must have been all but deserted that day. The Journal continued

. . . all the banks and manufacturers, and nearly the whole of the shops, were closed; little or no business of any kind transacted, and later most of the workmen were regaled at different public houses by their respective employers.

The canal was opened with panache and style. The committee of the Canal Co. joined a fleet of 14 vessels at Burgh. The fleet led by the 'Robert Burns', handsomely decorated and provided with an excellent band of music, proceeded to the canal basin where it was saluted by a 21-gun salute from the castle, then festivities were carried on into the evening and indeed all night. The *Journal* gave details.[49]

. . . soon after four o'clock the Committee, with white wands in their hands preceded by music, and accompanied by a multitude of people, walked in procession from the Canal Warehouses through Caldewgate, Abbey-street, Paternoster-row, Castle-street and English-street to the Bush Inn. There 150 gentlemen sat down to an elegant and sumptuous dinner.

The Committee now worked to build up a commercial trade. A timber-yard was built and timber rafts used on the canal. The Treasury waived coastal duties on coal, stone and slate carried between Whitehaven and Carlisle. Private enterprise was slow to make use of the canal and the Committee organised the first shipments. But soon business started to increase and anxiety arose

Bush Hotel coaching inn, demolished in 1817. The Hotel was rebuilt and re-orientated to open on to the viaduct. (*Tullie House*)

about the adequacy of the water from the reservoir. The problem was solved by the cutting of a feeder from the river and lifting the water to the canal by means of a water wheel.

In 1825 the newly formed Carlisle and Liverpool Steam Navigation Company was granted an exclusive berth at Port Carlisle, to be built by the Canal Company and repaid over ten years. The Company then bought the Bailie Nicol Jarvis, a second-hand packet boat, and offered it for lease. The combination of steam-boat in the Solway and packet-boat on the canal enabled passengers to leave Carlisle in the morning and arrive at Liverpool the same evening, a very competitive passenger service to the stage coaches operating on the turnpike roads. The passenger trade grew and the Solway Hotel was built at Port Carlisle for the entertainment of transit passengers and a second steam navigation company, the Carlisle, Annan and Liverpool started operation in 1833.[50] Parson and White list the services available from the canal basin:[51]

Liverpool – One vessel to and from Liverpool weekly (from a fleet of three vessels). In addition the 'Old Shipping Company' operated a boat to and from the dry docks, Liverpool, occasionally (with a fleet of three vessels).

Carlisle Canal, by M. Nutter, 1749–1832. (*County Library*)

Glasgow – One vessel to and from Glasgow regularly.

For passengers – The Canal Company's packet boat operated to and from Bowness three times a week during the five summer months.

Bowness to Liverpool – The Cumberland steam packet sailed from Bowness to Liverpool every Thursday and returned from Liverpool every Monday, and goods were conveyed along the canal to Bowness to meet the steam packet.

A major development in technology was taking place at this time, the introduction of steam driven sea going vessels, which was greatly to the advantage of the Canal Co. Up to 1826 sailing vessels alone passed between Carlisle and Liverpool, but in that year they were superseded by two steam vessels, the 'Solway' and the 'Cumberland' of 80 h.p. each, to be followed a few years later by the 'City of Carlisle' (120 h.p.), the 'Newcastle' (160 h.p.) and the 'Royal Victoria' (200 h.p.). One of the later boats was subsequently transferred to the Isle of Man and Belfast service. Independence of wind and weather greatly expedited the sea voyage and enabled a strict timetable to be kept.

It would be pleasant but misleading to picture a passenger packet boat sedately gliding down the canal. Sir George Head recalls the efforts of the owners of horse drawn canal boats to compete with steam.[52] The Arrow was a boat used by the Carlisle and Annan Navigation Company to convey their passengers to their two powerful steamers, the Newcastle and the City of Carlisle, waiting in the Firth to take them to Liverpool. The Arrow was built with a view to gliding through water with the utmost possible rapidity. It was a boat 66ft long and 5½ft wide, constructed from sheet iron, which drew only 9 inches of water when empty and when fully laden, with forty people and a good deal of baggage, only 12 inches. It was hauled down the canal by two high-blooded hunters, kept in prime condition and driven by a postilion on the hindmost horse, which cantered at 10 m.p.h. and performed the journey of 12 miles in 2 hours after negotiating six locks. Head notes '. . . though people were anxious to go on board her, she was to all appearance so cranky – toppling and rolling from side to side so awfully when empty, that folks took a panic and many declined on any account to venture.'

The fortunes of the Carlisle Canal Company must now be left to a later chapter and considered along with the development of the railways.

NOTES

1. Adam Smith, *The Wealth of Nations* (1776) Book I. Chapter 3, pp. 123–4.
2. Mannix and Whellan *History, Gazetteer and Directory of Cumberland* (1847), p. 38.
3. William Radcliffe, *Origin of the New System of Manufacturing called Power Loom Weaving* (1828; reprinted 1974), p. 58.
   The main textile areas, as listed by Radcliffe, were:
   (a) Manchester, with 30 to 50 miles in every direction round it.
   (b) Glasgow, extending to Perth, Aberdeen and a great part of the Highlands.
   (c) Nottingham, Derby, Warwick and Lichfield, etc.
   (d) Carlisle, branching out in every direction so as to meet the Manchester and Glasgow divisions.
4. 8 Geo. I c. 14. Bank End on the R. Eden is midway between the Solway and Carlisle.
5. Lord Harley, *Journey in England: Report on the Manuscripts of the Dukes of Portland,* Historical Manuscript Commission, pp. 129–32.
6. *The Cumberland Pacquet,* 9 May 1734.
7. L. A. Williams, *Road Transport in Cumberland in the Nineteenth Century* (1975) p. 38.
8. W. Lawson, *Construction of the Military Road in Cumberland 1751–58* T.C.W.A.A.S., New Series, LXXIX, p. 1.
9. 24 Geo. II c. 25.
10. Lawson, op. cit., p. 111.
11. The equivalent modern road is the B6264 Carlisle to Brampton and the 'top' road, the B6318, Greenhead to Heddon.
12. Lawson, op. cit., p. 118.
13. Mannix and Whellan, op. cit., p. 38.
14. 26 Geo. II c. 4. (modern road A6).
15. 26 Geo. II c. 31. (A66).
16. 26 Geo. II c. 16. (A6).
17. 26 Geo. II c. 50. (A65).

18. 26 Geo. II c. 13. (A595).

19. Mannix and Whellan, op. cit., p. 35.

20. L. A. Williams, op. cit., p. 32.

21. Ibid., p. 26.

22. R. G. Woodall, 'Carlisle Mails', *The Philatelist*, August 1950.

23. Woodall, op. cit.

24. *Cumberland Pacquet*, 14 May 1788.

25. *Universal British Directory* (1790), p. 631.

26. Hutchinson, op. cit., p. 666.

27. J. Bailey and G. Culley, *General View of Agriculture in Cumberland* (1794), p. 212.

28. J. Nicholson and R. Burns, *History and Antiquities of the Counties of Westmorland and Cumberland*, vol. 2 (1777), p. 11.

29. W. Wordsworth, *Guide to the Lakes* (5th edn, 1835).

30. *Universal British Directory* (1790), p. 623.

31. Adam Smith, *Wealth of Nations* (1776), Book I, Chapter 3, p. 122.

32. In a recent study, *The First Industrial Revolution*, Phyllis Deane quantifies the advantage of water transport in terms of the effective load a horse can draw, in tons, by different modes of transport. Thus: canal 50; navigable river 30; iron rails 8; macadam road 2; pack horse ⅛.

33. *William Chapman*, 1749–1832. An eminent engineer and friend of Watt and Matthew Boulton. A consultant engineer for many dock and canal schemes. He constructed canals in Ireland and docks in England and Scotland.

34. *Thomas Harrison*, 1744–1829. An architect, studied in Rome. Admitted to Academy of St Luke and awarded medals by Pope Clement XIV. He designed many buildings and re-built Chester Castle and designed the re-built Lancaster Castle. Built many bridges including the Grosvenor Bridge at Chester and the Skerton Bridge at Lancaster.

35. *Thomas Telford*, 1757–1834. Widely regarded as 'the greatest engineer of the age'. Built many major roads and bridges and canals.

36. William Chapman, *Survey of Line of Navigation from Newcastle-upon-Tyne to the Irish Channel* (1795).

37. William Chapman *Report on the Means of Obtaining a Safe and Commodious Communication From Carlisle to the Sea* (1807).

38. Thomas Harrison, *Report on the Select Committee of the Cumberland Navigation Canal* (1808).

39. Thomas Telford, *Report on the Intended Cumberland Canal* (1808).

40. Bewley Papers, *A Report on Meeting 11 August 1818* C.R.O., X/182/3, quoted by C. Hadfield & G. Bridle, *Canals of N.W. England*, vol. 2, p. 337.

41. W. Chapman, *Report on the Proposed Canal Navigation between Carlisle and the Solway Firth* (1818).

42. Ibid.

43. The subscriptions from the great landowners included Earl of Lonsdale £5,000, John Christian Curwen MP £1,000, Sir James Graham £1,000, Sir Philip Musgrave £500. Subscriptions from the Carlisle cotton industrialists included Peter Dixon and Sons £4,000, James and John Forster £2,000, J. R. & J. Ferguson £1,500, Richard and John Ferguson £500 each.

44. Total annual tonnage 73,749 which included Coal 29,549, Lime 15,000, Stone from Whitehaven 5,000, Slate 1,500, Cotton Wool 1,500, Cotton Yarn 1,500, Linen from Ireland 800, Grain 2,000, Timber 1,800, Manufactured Goods for export 1,000.

45. 59 Geo. III c. 13.

46. Ambiguity can occur when reading documents relating to Port Carlisle. In 1564–65 Carlisle was granted Port status. Carlisle was the port of Cumberland, while Whitehaven was but a member of Port Carlisle. In 1681 Whitehaven's increasing relative importance as a port was recognised by the grant of independent Port status. At a later date, with the development of traffic on the R. Eden, Sandsfield became known as Port Carlisle. With the construction of the canal, however, Fisher's Cross was to receive, and retain, the name of Port Carlisle.

47. *Carlisle Journal*, March 1823.

48. The total population of Carlisle at this time was about 16,000. It is evident that the opening ceremony of the canal must have dominated the lives of people in this city and in a considerable part of the surrounding countryside.

49. The location of the six-pounders was on the same site as that on which hostile batteries had been mounted, and directed against the city, in the 1745 rebellion.

50. I rely on C. Hadfield and G. Biddle, *Canals of N. W. England* vol. 2 (1970), pp. 341–2 for details of the early commercial activities of the Canal Company.

51. Parson and White *History, Directory and Gazetteer of Counties of Cumberland and Westmorland* (1829), p. 168.

52. Sir George Head, *A Tour through the Manufacturing Districts of England in 1835* pp. 345–51.

CHAPTER 2

The Growth of the
Factory System in Carlisle

The primary constraints on the development of Carlisle had now been alleviated, with the construction of the turnpike roads. Political conditions were stable and long distance transport for goods and people had been facilitated. In the second half of the eighteenth century a series of inventions in textile machinery was to transform the economy. The first faltering steps were made in the linen and woollen industries.

Hutchinson has recorded that German merchants from Hamburg had established a woollen manufactory in Carlisle by 1750 and under the supervision of the brothers Deulicher at first prospered, 'people up to a distance of 20 miles from the city were employed and every loom that could be got was put to work'. The products were broad and plain cloths with the firm processing the work from sheep shearing to the final product.[1] A snare however in reading early histories is that historical 'facts' are repeated, often word for word by successive historians, and repetition arouses a feeling of conviction that is not always justified, B. C. Jones has shown that entries in the Order Books of the city do not always tally with the account of Hutchinson's informant. It was Guliker brothers who leased from the corporation the Abbey Mill, which was situated on the Damside beneath the City West Walls, on 29 December 1724 to start up the woollen manufactory. The 'Old Dye House', or the fulling mill, was rebuilt at the Corporation's charge, but the firm went bankrupt in 1740.[2]

In 1750 R. & W. Hodgson started to manufacture a course linen cloth called Osnaburghs. Osnaburghs, a coloured stripe and check fabric, were exported to the southern parts of North America (the future USA) for the clothing of slaves, a favourable market, from its nature, stable and predictable and not subject to the vagaries of fashion. Two other businesses are worthy of note; the short-lived woollen manufactory of George Blamire and Richard Ferguson's linen business set up below the Town Hall in 1746. The woollen industry, however, soon faded out and was not to re-appear again until the cotton industry was in trouble 100 years later. Hutchinson writes '. . . from the time of the Deulichers, and the demise of the Blamire manufactory the business was no more pursued by any other adventurer.'[3]

From 1758 Carlisle received a big boost in consumer purchasing power. Some hundreds of French prisoners taken in the Seven Years War were sent

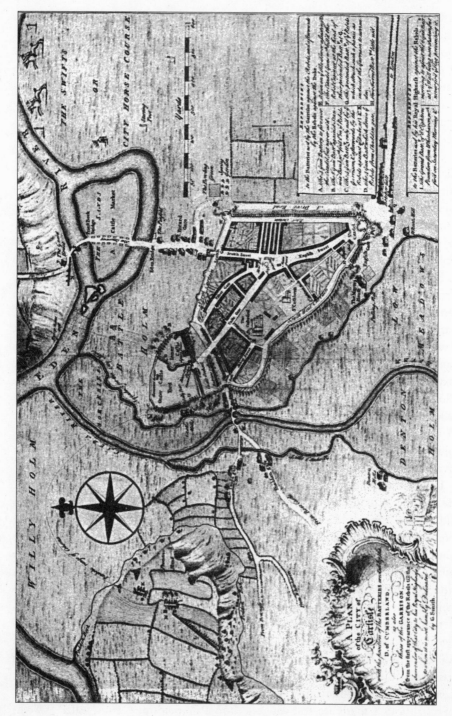

Map of Carlisle by G. Smith, 1746, showing the pre-industrial city. Note the Corporation dam supplying mills with water.

to Carlisle. Restrictions on their freedom do not appear to have been onerous. They were put on their parole of honour and each received 7s. a week allowance, generous indeed compared with the contemporary labourer's wage of 8d. to 10d. a day. In addition money circulation was stimulated by the stationing of the Westmorland Militia in the city. Hutchinson writes '. . . such a number of men in the city, and so well circumstanced as to money, greatly benefited the place. The consequences of this influx of wealth was the intro- duction of more expensive modes of living.'[4]

Technical innovations in the cotton industry were now to produce dramatic changes.[5] Kay's flying shuttle came into widespread use in the 1750s and 1760s, but its effect on the output of cloth was diminished by the bottleneck in the spinning branch of the industry. Notwithstanding, the Newcastle firm of Scot Lamb had the confidence to introduce a calico printing business into Carlisle in 1761 and they were soon to employ many hundreds of men, women and children. Machinery for the carding and spinning of cotton was now erected in different places in the neighbourhood of the city to compete, on favourable terms, with the cotton being supplied from Lancashire at great expense in carriage. Manufactories were now set up, notable Bernard Barton and Wood.[6] Barton was given permission by the corporation on 26 March 1764 'to erect a water wheel for washing and scouring of yarn or cloth on the mill race in Lamplugh Close'. Jones writes 'this was to mark the beginning of the new textile industry of calico printing on the site of the Long Island works. The Close had been let to Barton as a print field for a rent of £10 a year in 1762'.[7]

The bleaching process for cloth, associated with printing, was by exposure to the atmosphere, with rain and sun, combined with steepings in alkaline solutions. This was a very lengthy process. Baines gives a measure of the time involved.

The cloth was steeped in alkaline leys for several days, washed and then spread out on the grass for some weeks. The process was repeated five or six times and in total this could occupy six to eight months.[8] The large tracts of ground required for the spreading out of the cloth, and its lengthy exposure caused considerable pressure upon the available land. Hutchinson noted '. . . that the public works (for the cotton industry) occupied a great deal of good land about the city, so that the value of ground either in selling price or in letting rose considerably.'[9] Appendix 2 lists four printfields in the year 1794 which employed in total about 1,000 people. Inspection of the 1790 and 1805 maps (page 48) reveal two of these printfields, Lamb's on Corporation Dam and Donald's in Willow Holme. Not until the development of bleaching powder circa 1800 was it possible to supersede the crofting process and ease the pressure on land. It is significant that the term 'printfield' had disappeared from the Jollie 1811 map[10] although there are still references to Printfields at Cummersdale, Wood Bank and Denton Holme in the 1810 Directory.[11]

It is intriguing to speculate when the factory system for cotton spinning was introduced to Carlisle. Its feasibility stemmed from Arkwright's invention of the waterframe for spinning in 1769, which was widely adopted after the cancellation of his patents in 1785, and from his invention of ancillary machinery like the carding engine, to prepare the cotton wool for spinning, in 1775. These machines required more space than could be found in a cottage, more power than muscle power and their weight necessitated a strongly built mill. On the other hand on the weaving side of the industry factory mechanisation had to await until the next century. Hutchinson records that Messrs Wood employed about 200 people in the spinning of cotton, but no date is given and no reference made to a factory building,[12] and it seems possible that Wood was a co-ordinator of cottage jenny spinners rather than a mill owner. However, factories were beginning to make their appearance. Hutchinson wrote in 1794:

> The waters of the Caldew and Petterel [sic], and particularly the former, are remarkable for the quality of bleaching white. It is rather an unpleasant reflection, that these rapid streams, so peculiarly adapted for the purpose of turning machinery, for miles above Carlisle, more particularly the Caldew: and by proper application of which, the city might be rendered almost the Birmingham of the north, should only be employed in giving motion to three or four solitary corn mills, and a few cotton works.[13]

Forster, at Cummersdale, and the Fergusons, at Warwick Bridge, however undoubtedly used water power and erected substantial mills and unequivocally can be counted among the pioneers of the factory system at Carlisle. Records are available to follow the progress of these firms from the last decade of the eighteenth century and the early years of the nineteenth century, and to gain an insight into the organisation and the evolving technology of the early cotton industry.

Langthwaite Mill

John, Richard and George, the three sons of the late Richard Ferguson who had set up the linen business in 1746, leased a six acre site at Warwick Bridge in 1790, erected a mill, built a 700 yard mill-race, to harness the Cairn Beck and erected a water-wheel.[14] Adjacent to the mill warehouses and dyehouses were erected. A series of events were now to occur that provide documentary evidence of the technology of the spinning mill at this time, the transition from muscle-powered spinning jennies to water powered waterframes and carding engines, and the transformation from a cottage scale industry to a true factory.

The mill was destroyed by fire on 8 August 1793. The *Cumberland Pacquet* of the following week reported that the main mill building was gutted, the

Langthwaite Mill, built by Ferguson in 1790. The mill was rebuilt after a fire in 1795 (the three-storey building on the right of the picture). In 1809 it was leased to Dixon, who extended with the new four-storey mill to the left.

raw cotton and the jenny wheel destroyed, but almost the whole of the twist and spun cotton and some frames of the carding engine were saved from the flames and the great water-wheel preserved.[15] The wording of the report strongly suggests that complementary use of the spinning jenny to spin the cotton weft, and the water-powered carding engine and waterframes to produce cotton twist (warp). The company was fully insured and the Fergusons were able to rebuild and re-equip their mill. The new mill was massive by the standards of the day measuring 66' × 33' in plan, contained three floors and an attic.[16] The Fergusons carried on the business until 1809 when they leased the mill to their brother-in-law Peter Dixon and his sons. The industrial historian is again fortunate in that an inventory of the factory machinery has survived and shows the very latest spinning machinery, the mules and the 'water throstles' were installed in the 1790s to supplement the earlier waterframes and spinning jennies, a most comprehensive collection of the machines that transformed the cotton industry. An interpretation of the use of the various machines at this time is given in Appendix No. 3.

Now the original three storey mill was extended with a new wing of four storeys and an attic, and a new reservoir was built to increase the water supply.[17] In 1832 a steam engine was installed to supplement the power supply and make it secure at times of low water, an early recourse to steam power made economic by the opening of the Carlisle Canal in 1823. But the firm had made earlier recourse to coal with the installation of a gas house and of gas lighting in the

Shaddon Mill, built by Dixons, 1836.

factory, and when James Losh visited the factory in 1826 he reported that the works operated twenty-four hours a day. 'The day labourer working from 6 a.m. to 7.30 p.m. and the night labourer 7.30 p.m. to 6 a.m.'[18]

When Dixons erected their Shaddon Mills in Carlisle in 1836 they made an abortive attempt to sell Langthwaite Mill. A sale notice refers to the imminent opening of the Newcastle–Carlisle Railway, to an adjacent coal depot, to dye houses capable of containing 130 vats, to a bleach house, and to thirty-four cottages, a gas house and accommodation for a steam engine.[19] Clearly the factory was keeping abreast of new technology at that time with steam power and gaslighting and indoor bleaching processes superseding the old crofting methods. The Langthwaite Mill prospered. Additional new plant was installed, and by 1847 the firm employed 320 hands.

The disasters which were to befall the Dixon firm in the 1860s and the bankruptcy in 1877 are related below, but first of all reference will be confined to the Langthwaite Mill and its position at that time as revealed in a report in the *Cumberland Pacquet* in 1873.[20] 'Although the Mill itself was idle the adjoining dye and bleach works, containing over 300 iron dyeing vats, and 17 indigo mills drive by a condensing engine, a water-wheel and two turbines,[21] were fully employed on finishing work for the firm's Carlisle factories.'[22]

The Langthwaite mill had now been reduced to a finishing factory. With the collapse of the Dixon firm the golden age of the cotton trade in Carlisle was over. Langthwaite ceased to trade in 1883.

John Forster

John Forster was an outstanding example of the industrial entrepreneur at the turn of the century. He was a Carlisle banker who build up inter-related cotton enterprises. He owned a cotton mill at Cummersdale in the 1790s operated by John Forster and Sons, Robert Pattinson and others. In 1801 he built a print works also at Cummersdale, operated by Forster, James and Company; later by Forster, James, Wastell, Donald & Company; but this business was closed down in 1817.[23] Hutchinson's report in 1794 that 'Forster had the most extensive manufactory in the north of England in all branches of the cotton industry starting from the raw material to the finishing of checks, calicoes and muslins,'[24] suggests that Forster was involved in the printing and finishing trade int he city prior to the opening of the Cummersdale Print Works on 1801. One might speculate that it was the same Forster who was the partner in the Lamb, Scot and Forster Printfield listed by Hutchinson in 1794.[25]

Although Forster built his Cummersdale print works some years after the development of bleaching powder the firm was firmly rooted in the old crofting processes. A report of a court case reveals that John Mattinson, a labourer, was apprehended in possession of a piece of white calico 'in a damp state as if taken from a bleaching ground.' Such was the severity of the penal code at that time that Mattinson was sentenced to seven years' transportation.[26]

John Forster died in 1827. His Will showed him to be an entrepreneur with a wide range of business interests and assets including the former printworks (Forster, James and Company); a water cornmill occupied by John Dalton, a cotton mill (Forster, Pattinson and others); a farm in the occupation of John Nixon; weaving sheds at Brampton occupied by John Clementson; the banking concern of Thomas Forster & Company. In addition he bought shares in the Carlisle Navigation Company and in the Carlisle Gas and Coke Works.[27]

After Forster's death the mill at Cummersdale remained unused until 1835 when it was taken over by Thomas McAlpin, of whom more will be written later.

By the end of the eighteenth century other important Carlisle firms appeared on the scene. In 1780 the iron founding firm of Porter Hinde & Porter was set up in Blackfriars Street. This firm was to develop an important trade in bar-iron with shipping concerns operating from North West England, Scotland and Ireland. The Old and New Breweries in Caldewgate, Iredales off James St and one other smaller brewery built when formerly the publicans brewed their own ale using their hand mills to grind the malt. Other cotton spinners were established[28] and two banks were founded to service the burgeoning capitalist economy. As a portent of important things to come, in 1799 Benjamin Scott announced that he '. . . was commending business as a printer, bookseller, stationer and patent medicine vendor in a commodious house in the market place.'[29] An inauspicious start to the metal box and printing industry of later years.

Hutchinson was too near to appreciate fully the scale of the changes that were now occurring in the city. He described Carlisle as a frontier town '. . . fortified with a wall and a citadel and a castle kept still in some sort of repair,[30] but he did not perhaps give sufficient weight to the fine detail that he had meticulously recorded in his inventory of manufacturers in the city.[31] The character of Carlisle, in 1790, was clearly changing from a 'frontier' town to an industrial city dependent upon, and supplying, the outside world.

Major Carlisle cotton firms of the nineteenth century

The 1820s saw a rapid acceleration in the growth of the UK cotton industry. Large new factories were being built and water and steam power were replacing human muscle. Graph No. 2 shows the exponential growth of raw cotton consumption in the United Kingdom and the sharp rise in the number of factory workers in the industry. The adoption of power looms halted the growth of, and impoverished, the domestic hand-loom weaver and within a decade their numbers dramatically decreased.[32] It is in this national context that a study has been made of three major Carlisle textile firms of the nineteenth century.

Fergusons (Holme Head)

Two generations of the Ferguson family have already been mentioned. Richard Ferguson who started up a linen business in the mid-eighteenth century and his sons who introduced, on a major scale, cotton spinning at Warwick Bridge. Now in the third generation Joseph Ferguson, a grandson of Richard, started the dyeing and finishing of cotton goods in 1824 at the Friggate works on the old mill race some 500 yards north of the present Holme Head Works.[33]

Joseph Ferguson introduced the idea of beetling the cotton cloth in a similar way to that of linen. The process involved the rapid and repeating pounding

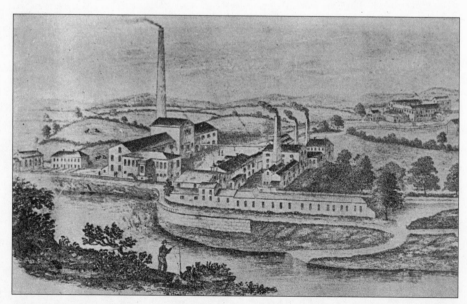

Fergusons' Holme Head cotton mill, *c.* 1854. (*Tullie House*)

Fergusons'
Holme Head
cotton mill
as it was in
1928.
(*Carlisle
Journal*, 1928)

Joseph Ferguson (1787–1863), the grand-
son of the founder, Richard. He opened
Friggate Works in 1824, purchased the
Holme Head site in 1852 and was Mayor
in 1836–37 and MP 1852–57.
(*Tullie House*)

of the cloth by rows of wooden full-
ers to produce a soft silky finish. The
product, 'Silesias' as he named it,
gained immediate success especially
in the United States and he was soon
encouraged to rent a mill at Holme
Head (1828) previously occupied by
Garrick and Johnston, the cotton
spinners. The firm continued to
prosper and in 1837 he built a new
works for dyeing and finishing cotton fabrics, in 1852 he completed the
purchase of the Holme Head Estate
and the firm prospered in the finishing processes of the cotton industry.
Joseph Ferguson took a paternal interest in his employees and built cottages and provided allotments for
their use and founded a mixed school
– the Robert Ferguson School.
Joseph died in 1863 and was succeeded by his son Robert who carried on the family business. Robert
had political interests and was mayor
of the city in 1836/7 and MP for
Carlisle in 1852–7. In 1865 the Chance family injected new capital in the firm
and in 1870 Frederick Chance became Managing Director. The firm now
erected a spinning mill and a weaving shed at Holme Head and pioneered
new systems of dyeing and finishing, to enable it to become a fully integrated
cotton manufacturer.[34] An act of courage after the cotton famine consequent
upon the American Civil War.

Peter Dixon

The early history of Langthwaite Mill up to 1809 when Peter Dixon and his
sons took over the ownership from Ferguson Bros., has been reviewed. Now
in 1836 the Dixons erected the magnificent Shaddon Mills, a building of seven
storeys with ground dimensions of 224 × 58ft and a chimney rising to 305ft.

It contained a large engine house and a boiler house with seven boilers. A
factory of this size could not have been operated with the available water power
and steam power was employed from the beginning. Coal from West Cumberland could be imported to the nearby canal basin and within two years an
alternative supply would be available, at the same terminus, from the Carlisle

and Newcastle railway. The firm Peter Dixon and Sons was to become a major industrial enterprise. Mannix and Whellan claim that the firm '. . . alone gives employment in the various departments of their cotton works to about 8,000 hands.'[35] Dixons, of course, had the considerable factory at Warwick Bridge besides their Carlisle Works and they made great use of the hand loom weavers, a family employment occupying men, women and children in loom shops fitted into their own cottages. By the 1840s '. . . most of the streets in the vicinity of Shaddongate were inhabited principally by factory hand hand loom weavers and textile finishers.'[36] But the catchment area for hand

George (1793–1860) and Mary Dixon. George was the son of Peter Dixon senior. He lived at Blencogo and Tullie House, and was mayor in 1842–43 and 1848–49. (*Tullie House*)

loom weavers was much wider '. . . and included villages surrounding Carlisle within a radius of twenty miles.'[37] The weavers collected their yarn from Dixons and delivered their product weekly to the Peter Street Warehouse. The cottage weaving industry was augmented in the 1840s. 'Messrs Dixon have laid alongside their great factory a commodious building in which several hundred power looms give work to a large number of our population.'[38] The hand loom weavers were still there in the 1860s, but '. . . the trade was then decaying.'[39] Once the industrialists started to build their own loom shops and used direct labour, the days of the cottage industry were numbered. The fully integrated cotton manufacturer would eventually destroy the cottage industry.

But the Dixon firm was to meet disaster in the 1860s. First the supply of American raw cotton was cut off by the Civil War (1861–65). Subsequently the freeing of the American slaves adversely affected Dixon's trade. Bulmer in 1884 wrote:

> The golden age of the cotton trade in Carlisle fell with the abolition of slavery in America. Formerly every great slave plantation took a large quantity of ginghams for its negroes, and always adhered to the same pattern . . . but the free negro demands a gaudier article; he is capricious, and must be ticked and attracted by new patterns. This altered state of things the Carlisle

spinners have, from various causes, been unable to adapt themselves to, and it seems probable that the trade will shortly leave Carlisle.[40]

The supplanting of hand loom weaving by the factory system put Dixons at a further disadvantage because of their previous reliance on the cottage industry.[41] In 1872 the partners Peter James Dixon, John Dixon and Joseph Forster were declared bankrupt. There was a rescue attempt and a short reprieve. A new joint stock company, Peter Dixon & Sons Ltd on the 20 January 1873 acquired both the Langthwaite Mill and the Carlisle factories, but the firm ceased to trade in 1883.[42] A great pioneering cotton firm was disastrously overtaken by its innate conservatism and unpredictable political events.

Stead and McAlpin of Cummersdale[43]

The origin of this Cummersdale industry can be traced back to 1790 when Brownwell and Irving established a manufactury for printed textiles half a mile outside Wigton (said variously to be at Spittal and/or Burnfoot). By 1811 the business was managed by Ferguson and Irving and by 1821 was known as Messrs Ferguson, Halliley & Co, and was managed by Halliley and Thomas McAlpin. The Wigton works were known as the Stampery and employed some fifty men. Thomas McAlpin and three brothers and nephew Hugh who were also calico printers, left Wigton in 1835 and took over a disused mill at Cummersdale which had been vacated by Forster in 1817. There were 21 hand printers and 7 indigo pencillers who came with the business from Wigton. It

Cammersdale print works, painting by Sam Bough, *c.* 1835. The factory was erected in 1801 and operated by John Forster until 1817. It was repaired and taken over by Thomas McAlpin in 1835. (*Tullie House*)

is said that they walked the 12 miles from Wigton to Cummersdale with their property and tools on their backs and in carts.

McAlpin repaired and renovated the buildings and equipped the mill with a new water-wheel for driving the machinery and installed engraved copper rollers for printing. A partial bill from James Houtson of Manchester for the re-fitting of the mill in 1835 exists.[44] In a total expenditure of £1,332, £200 was spent on a 'four coloured cylinder printing machine on the newest and most improved principles.' Other items on the Bill were dye cisterns, squeezers, mangle calender, drum wash wheels and a stretching machine. A considerable sum was paid to mill-wrights for the erection of shafting and gearing to drive the machines. Other items included steam chests (drying cylinders) for process work, an indigo mill and a number of copper cylinders.

The re-equipment schedule shows a comparatively late adoption of the cylindrical roller printer that had been invented by Bell half a century earlier, and that the company did not choose to employ steam power although the technology was now available, as was an economic coal supply. Although the copper rollers for printing opened up a vast market for mass production there was still a niche in the market for the variety and beauty of the hand-block printed fabrics, so that the two technologies existed side by side up to very recent times.

In 1843 when Forster went bankrupt Thomas McAlpin bought the mill that he had formerly leased.[45] The sale notice for the property states '. . . the machinery was driven by a never failing stream of the purest water which runs through the centre of the premises . . .'[46] which may have been sufficient reason for the retention of water power. The notice also lists a bleaching ground which suggests that the crofting process may still have been in use nearly half a century after the introduction of bleaching powder.

John Stead, a stepson of Thomas McAlpin was brought into the business, probably in 1837, and the firm continued to prosper. A London office and a warehouse at Cheapside were set up permitting a direct contact with retailers in the London and International market. With the coming of the railways the demands of contemporary fashion and popular taste were to become an important factor in the economic development of the firm.

On the death of Thomas McAlpin in 1849 the firm became known as McAlpin, Stead and Company and soon received national recognition. It exhibited at the Great Exhibition of 1851 and in 1862 they won gold medals at the International Exhibition at Hyde Park for block-printed chintz. The firm was now employing highly skilled craftsmen in the art of transforming designs to rollers, and blocks, and using the service of gifted artists to product a product of beauty an charm, qualities which one does not normally associate with the industrial revolution. A book containing photographs taken from the original printed fabrics attests to the artistic merit of the company's products.[47]

In 1867 John Stead became sole proprietor and changed the name of the firm to Stead McAlpin and Co. By 1868 the company had assets of £25,000, employed 200 hands and was the only surviving print works in Cumberland. The firm continued to thrive though this review must finish at the mid nineteenth century. The study of the companies records gives a fascinating picture of old and new technologies existing side by side, the opening up of Carlisle to the national and international market, and of a firm that became a leader in its field.

The dynamic growth of 3 major Carlisle textile firms has been reviewed in this chapter, but pertinent questions remain to be answered. How did these firms, from modest beginnings, build up the financial resources to erect the equip their massive new factories. How for instance did the Dixons mobilise the resources to extend their vast cotton enterprise which culminated in their show piece, the magnificent Shaddon mills.

The problem will be looked at in some detail. Firstly, in a national context, on the constraints on the raising of capital by industrial entrepreneurs in the eighteenth/nineteenth centuries; secondly in a local context, where however the information is limited because of the essentially private nature of the negotiation of loans when the facilities for the raising of share capital, or commercial long term loans, were so limited. A subsidiary theme will be the development of the banking system. Its importance to the Carlisle industrialist is emphasised by the fact that some of the early bankers were the cotton entrepreneurs. The industrialist had two problems, long and short term. First, long term finance to set up and extend his factory. Second, to provide working capital. The first constraint on the raising of capital was legislative. The industrialist had been effectively prohibited from raising money on the stock exchange for factory building by legislation, dating back to 1719, enacted to curb the speculation excesses in the second decade of the eighteenth century.[48] Two great trading companies, the East Indian Co. and the South Sea Co., were explicitly excluded from the proscription in the 1719 Act, and it is ironic in the next year the latter company collapsed. The constraints on the raising of capital in the aftermath of the South Sea Bubble were to continue into the next century, unless the borrowers were to incur the cost, and uncertainty, of promoting a Special Act of Parliament. The restrictions were eventually lifted in 1825,[49] but with a proviso that future charters should be conditional upon members of a Corporation being individually liable in their persons and property for any debt, or contracts, of the Corporation. The absence of a limited liability clause made an industrial investment decidedly unattractive for a private investor and inevitably it was left to the committed partners in an enterprise to shoulder all the risk and to raise capital from their own resources, or by seeking personal loans at a fixed rate of interest.

The second constraint was that eighteenth-century banks were not structured to provide the long-term loans necessary for industrial development. Provincial banks had arisen directly from the demands of merchants and industrialists for short term accommodation. They serviced bills of exchange[50] and provided a discount service for the merchant wishing to get back into cash before the maturing of the bill. The early banking services were frequently run by the merchant, or industrialist, who besides organising his own financial transactions, offered his services to fellow merchants for their mutual convenience and profit. London banks served as agents of the country banks to handle the flow of bills of exchange transferred to the capital. They provided the country bank with currency, in notes or coins, for the ever increasing wage earning population, and they covered the bank, when necessary, with overdraft facilities.

The names of the early Carlisle bankers are indicative of the section of the community from which they came. The first two Carlisle banks established in the middle of the eighteenth century by Messrs Forster and Son, and Mr Wilson, 'were of considerable service to the growing trade of the city.'[51] In 1790 the bankers were John Forster, Sons, James and Co, and Messrs Liddell, Losh, Staples, Ferguson & Co.[52] John Forster's Will mentioned earlier confirms the connection between banker and industrialist, and the names of the other bankers strongly suggest a connection with Carlisle cotton entrepreneurs. By 1829 there were 5 banks in the city[53] who facilitated cash transactions and created credit for business interests. In 1837 there was a significant change in the City's banking system. The banks were no longer just an appendage of a merchant or industrialist firm, but specialised businesses in their own right. Seven banks were listed in the Directory, including the Carlisle and Cumberland Joint Stock Bank, the Carlisle District Bank, the Carlisle Borough Bank and significantly a Savings Bank,[54] a sign of the growing spread of savings among Carlisle citizens and an acquired confidence to induce them to deposit their savings. Each bank had a London Correspondent through which large-scale business could be transacted. As corporate banks they were able to attract capital and make loans to a variety of industries.

A distinction can now be made between the industrialist seeking short term loans, and the factory building industrialist requiring a long term credit to bridge the long gap before his investment could generate profits. Early cotton entrepreneurs, served by existing banks, were merchants and machinery renters who supplied the cottage operatives with a hand loom or spinning jenny. The big cotton merchant would require considerable resources to finance his business while the cotton was in the pipeline. He would import his raw cotton from America, via Liverpool, and transport it to his own warehouse. The cotton would be processed through its several stages to the finished product during which time he would pay the operatives weekly for their labour. Then the goods would be transported to the great cotton market of Manchester for national, and international, distribution before he could be repaid for his outlay. For a firm like Dixons, with their thousands of outworkers, the bridging finance would have been very considerable. But there were comparatively short term capital requirements which were successfully met by the existing banking and credit facilities.

The merchant, however, who became manufacturers required long term finance which mercantile financial institutions could not meet. They would now have to rely on their trading profits, and savings ploughed back into the business, or commonly, they would turn to kinsmen, or fellow industrialists, for long term loans. The rise of the great Dixon enterprise provides and example. Peter Dixon, with his sons, became manufacturers when he leased the Longthwaite mill in 1809 from his brothers-in-law, and fellow entrepreneurs, the Ferguson brothers, and the Dixon sons made a major extension to the factory in 1816 with the aid of a loan of £6,694 from their uncle George Ferguson.[55] One can marvel at the heroic scale of their next project, and give full recognition to the courage and imagination of the Dixons, when they built Shaddon mills in 1836, but one must also remember that the factory was but one aspect of their business. They were by now powerful merchants concerned with the buying of raw cotton, and the marketing of the finished article, be it the product of the factory or the domestic cottage weaver. They were men of substance and had the resources in 1818 to subscribe £4,000 towards the building of the Carlisle Canal. Even after the massive Shaddon cotton spinning mill was in operation the industrial and mercantile activities went on side by side and complemented one another, and it is reasonable to suppose that the resources of the merchant backed those of the industrialist.

One other question remains. Where did the labour force come from to man the factories, and the domestic hand loom and spinning wheel? Or to go one stage further back, what was the source of the greatly expanded Carlisle population which increased from just over 4,000 in 1765 to nearly 22,000 in

1841? It cannot be accounted for by an increasing birth rate, or a decreasing death rate, which in fact increased from 2.5% in the 1780s to 2.72% in the 1840s. One major influence must be the massive immigration of poverty stricken Irish and Scots seeking employment in the early decades of the nineteenth century. How this changed the ethnic base of the Carlisle population will be discussed in more detail in Chapter 3. The other major factor was the agricultural revolution, if it may be so called, with the enclosure of land by the landowners, with greater efficiency and labour saving and the inevitable displacement of cottagers and small farmers who sought employment in the booming textile industry.

The progress of the enclosure movement in North Cumberland is documented in the journals of travellers through Cumberland. Celia Fiennes travelled from Penrith to Carlisle in 1698 on her way to Scotland. She painted a picture of primitive agriculture:

> The ways [from Penrith] to Carlisle over much heath – you pass by little hutts and hovels the poor live in like barnes, some have them daub'd with mud wall others dye walls.[56]

The next report is from Sir John Clark, on his journeys from Carlisle to Penrith in 1721, who noted some limited enclosure:

> . . . the ground to the west was a fine country, all enclosed after the English way . . . these inclosures tho' they are not perfectly fencible, yet they beautify the country and keep the ground warm and distinguished in their marches . . . to the east for the most part there are only wild moor and commons . . .[57]

In 1771, Arthur Young[58] supplies an abundance of agricultural information as he travels from Scotland, through Brampton to Carlisle, Penrith and Kendal, and on the road from Penrith to Keswick, he notes the undeveloped land. Thus, north of Brampton, this land was an excellent sandy land but quite uncultivated. The country, between Penrith and Keswick . . . much of it moors and quite uncultivated, though evidently capable of it. Between Penrith and Shap, there was both enclosed and unenclosed land. From Shap to Kendal the land was totally unenclosed.

The remaining land from Brampton–Carlisle–Penrith–Shap, one must infer, for the absence of comment, was enclosed. This is confirmed by this description given of farms on this route, mixed farms with arable and pasture. The cereal crops included, wheat, oats and barley but with wheat omitted between Penrith and Shap. The enclosure movement accelerated between 1763 and 1800 and 40,000 acres of Cumberland was enclosed.[59] Under the act of 1801, common rights were lost and land re-apportioned between great estates. Nevertheless, the land was beautified by hedges and the stone walls on the mountains gave a dramatic effect.

The change to land use was stimulated by pioneering agriculturists such as Philip Howard of Corby Castle, John Christian Curwen of West Cumberland, Sir James Graham of Netherby and Lord Lonsdale of Lowther. The large scale enclosures and the introduction of new machinery greatly increased efficiency and the ability to feed the rapidly increasing population of the towns. The downside was that the small farmer and crofter could no longer make a living. There was an exodus to the towns to provide a labour force for industry and for the increasing demand for labour for the construction of roads, canals and railways.

NOTES

1. W. Hutchinson, *History of the County of Cumberland*, vol. 2 (1794), p. 660.
2. B. C. Jones, 'Carlisle's First Factory', *T.C.W.A.A.S.* (1985).
3. Hutchinson, op. cit., p. 662.
4. Hutchinson, op. cit., p. 663.
5. Appendix No. 1 provides a chronology and short description of the cotton industry processes and machinery.
6. Hutchinson, op. cit., p. 663–4.
7. Jones, op. cit.
8. E. Baines, *History of Cotton Manufacturer in Great Britain* (1835) (republished 1966), p. 246.
9. Hutchinson, op. cit., p. 663.
10. Map 1811.
11. See Appendix No. 4.
12. Hutchinson, op. cit., p. 664.
13. Hutchinson, op. cit., p. 679.
14. D. J. W. Mawson, 'Langthwaite Cotton Mill', *T.C.W.A.A.S.,* New Series, LXXVI (1976).
15. *Cumberland Pacquet*, August 1793.
16. Photograph.
17. Mawson, op. cit., pp. 164–7.
18. Losh MSS, quoted by Mawson, op. cit., p. 168.
19. *Carlisle Journal*, 16 January 1836, quoted by Mawson, op. cit., p. 168.
20. *Cumberland Pacquet*, 7 January 1873.
21. Many water turbines were being installed in mills in England in the second half of the nineteenth century. As compared with the water-wheel their smaller size and very much higher speeds, made them very suitable for fast running machinery. Many existing water-wheels were replaced by turbines which could easily be fitted in the same pit and use the same head and tail races.
22. The Carlisle factories included the Shannon Mills and weaving shops. But Bulmers Directory of 1884 also refers to large works in Peter Street and Tait Street.
23. Inf. Allan James.
24. Hutchinson, op. cit., p. 664.
25. Appendix No. 2.

26. *Carlisle Jounal*, 18 January 1817.

27. Carlisle Record Office DRC/2 (Dalson Court Leet and Baron Book 1817–1846).

28. See Appendix No. 4.

29. *Cumberland Pacquet*, 1799, quoted by G. Topping, *Memories of Old Carlisle*, p. 187.

30. Hutchinson, op. cit., p. 658.

31. See Appendix No. 4.

32. The graph of the number of factory workers employed shows some discontinuity between 1823 and 1830. It seems probable that a number of large factory units were commissioned in that period, and an attempt has been made to smooth out the curve. The raw cotton consumption curve, has been smoothed as only the trend of increase in cotton consumption consequent upon the growth of the factory system is of immediate interest.

33. *Centenary Ferguson Brothers Carlisle (1824–1924)* provides much of the information used in this section.

34. *Centenary Ferguson Brothers Carlisle.*

35. Mannix and Whellan *History, Gazetteer & Directory of Cumberland* (1847) p. 166. This astonishing claim is quoted, in similar terms, in later works, but no independent confirmation has been found. But it is known from the Muggeridge Report of 1840 that Dixons at that time employed approximately 1,200 hand loom weavers in Scotland and Ireland. W. Whellan in his 1860 Directory stated that Dixons '. . . by its extent rivals some of the largest in Lancashire.'

36. A. Harris, 'Denton Holme', Part 2, *T.C.W.A.A.S.*, New Series, LXVII, p. 211.

37. *Centenary Ferguson Brothers*, p. 81.

38. W. Whellan, *History of Cumberland & Westmorland* (1860), p. 97.

39. J. Walter Brown, *Round Carlisle Cross* (1928), 8th Service, p. 39.

40. T. Bulmer, *History and Directory of East Cumberland* (1884), p. 52.

41. *Centenary Ferguson Bros.*, p. 22.

42. D. J. W. Mawson, *Langthwaite Cotton Mill T.C.W.A.A.S.*, vol. 76, New Series, p. 171.

43. Much of the information for this section on Stead and McAlpin has been obtained from the John Lewis Partnership archives, complemented by information on Cummersdale industries from *Mr Allan James*, local historian.

44. *Archives of John Lewis Partnership.*

45. See photograph.

46. *Carlisle Journal*, 18 October 1843.

47. C. G. E. Bunt and E. A. Rose , *Two Centuries of English Chintz* (1957).

48. The Act of 1719 (6 Geo. 1 c 18) granted charters for the formation of two companies for the 'Assurance of Ships and Merchandise at Sea' and for lending money upon Bottomry.' But the relevance of the Act for the present chapter was that it proscribed the formation of other companies. Such undertaking, which encouraged speculation by the public were deemed to be public nuisances 'which manifestly tend to the common grievance, prejudice and inconvenience of great numbers of your Majesty's subjects in their trade or commerce and other [of] their affairs; and the persons who contrive or attempt such dangerous and mischievous Undertakings or Projects under false pretences of publick good, according to their own devices and schemes, to open public subscriptions and draw in many unwary

persons to subscribe therein towards raising great sums of money . . . [and in many cases] have presumed to act as if they were corporate bodies, and have pretended to make their shares in stocks transferable or assignable without any legal authority either by Act of Parliament or by any Charter from the Crown for so doing . . .'

49. 6 Geo. IV c 91.

50. Bills of exchange were in effect IOUs, whereby debtors could delay payment for 3, 6 or 12 months ahead. This was an early form of currency which could be transferred from hand to hand. Traders could sell them at a discount to meet their urgent requirements, e.g. to pay wages.

51. Parson and White *History, Directory and Gazetteer of Counties of Cumberland and Westmorland* (1829), p. 153.

52. *Universal British Directory* (1790), p. 630.

53. Parson and White, op. cit., p. 153.

54. 1837 Directory, p. 37

55. Mawson, op. cit., p. 166.

56. Celia Fiennes, *Illustrated Journey 1682–1712*. Ed. Christopher Morris.

57. Prevost W.A.J., 'A journey to Carlisle and Penrith – Sir John Clerk 1741'. *T.C.W.A.A.S.*, New Series, LXI, p. 202.

58. Arthur Young, *Six Months Tour Through the North of England* (1771), vol. 3. Letter XVI.

59. W. Rollinson, *A History of Cumberland and Westmorland* (1978), p. 87.

CHAPTER 3

Booming Carlisle
and an Alternative Economy

This island is pre-eminent among civilised nations for the prodigious development of its factory wealth, and has therefore been long viewed with a jealous admiration by foreign powers.

Andrew Ure[1]

> I'm a poor cotton weaver as many one knows
> I've nowt to eat i'th house an I've worn out my clos,
> You'd hardly give sixpence for all I have on
> My clogs are brossen, and stockings I've none,
> You'd think it was hard to be sent into th' world
> To clem and do th' best ot you con . . .

Early nineteenth–century ballad[2]

The industrial revolution in Carlisle rapidly gained impetus in the first quarter of the nineteenth century. In retrospect, after the elapse of nearly two centuries, this period is seen as a time of expansion, when the industrial base was formed on which a more affluent society could be built, when Carlisle was transformed from a medieval type walled city to a rapidly expanding open city, with fine new buildings and a more elegant life style for the more favoured citizens, and with a linkage to the rest of the country by regular coach and waggon services. But there was no ordered premeditated process in Carlisle for the formation of a better society able to benefit from the increased wealth that was being created. One perspective of this complex picture shows economic growth and the creation of wealth but another and less pleasing perspective shows a deeply divided society where large sections of the population, having lost the meagre independence they formerly possessed, had become pauperised. The two perspectives of economic growth, material plenty and urban renaissance in the more prestigious parts of the city, and its apparent antithesis of poverty, destitution and degeneration must each be given full weight if an authentic picture of Carlisle of the early nineteenth century is to be obtained. An earlier chapter has recorded the introduction of the factory system, for the spinning of cotton, into Carlisle, but now more must be said about the transformation of the industry due to the vastly increased scale of the production of yarn now possible, and how this upset the earlier balance between the output of the spinner and the capacity of the weaver, initially to his benefit but ultimately, with new immigration factors coming into play, to his destruction.

In 1770 the output of the cottage weaver was limited by the quantity of yarn he could procure. Radcliffe[3] drew attention to the great back up assistance it required to keep one weaver busy at his loom

> but the great sheet anchor of all cottages, and small farms, was the labour attached to the hand wheel, and when it is considered that it required 6 to 8 hands to prepare and spin yarn – sufficient for the consumption of one weaver, this shows clearly the inexhaustible source there was for every person from the age of 7 to 80 years (who retained their sight and could move their hands) to earn their bread, say 1 to 3 shillings per week without going to the parish.[4]

But now technical innovation was about to transform the industry. Hargreaves' spinning jenny, patented in 1770, multiplied many times the output of the spinner. Initially 4 spindles were accommodated on each set of gearing, but eventually large frames, with multiples of 4 spindles, reached a total of 80 spindles. The yarn produced on the jenny was soft, suitable only for weft, but within a few years the introduction of Arkwright's water frame produced a strong cotton twist suitable for warp. When Arkwright's patents were cancelled in 1785 water frames were made with as many as 48 spindles, increasing possibly to 100 by the year 1800. The water frame, dependent upon water power as the name implies, took twist production from the cottage to the factory.[5]

By the 1780s the use of the Jenny and water frame, complemented by the flying shuttle on the loom invented half a century earlier, permitted the manufacture of cheap calicoes which replaced linen and woollen goods. Another major technical innovation, the Mule, the mating of a Jenny with a water frame, which had appeared by the end of the century, was capable of producing both the warp and weft of every cloth from the finest muslin to the heaviest fustian which, by giving a superabundance of yarn, put the pressure on the weaver to keep up.

Radcliffe, giving evidence to a Committee of the House of Commons in 1808, reported on the transformation in the industry which the development of machinery for spinning cotton had produced during the 9 years from 1793–1802; it had

> become so perfect as to enable the spinner to produce more yarn than could at that time possibly be made into cloth by all the weavers of Great Britain could collect for that purpose. The demand for cotton goods was equal during this period to take off the whole produce of the spindles, could weavers have been found to make it into cloth.[6]

The golden age for the hand loom weaver had dawned and he now reached the zenith of his fortunes. A paraphrase of Radcliffe's account describes how:

every lumber room, barn and outbuilding was used for the installation of additional looms; when available room was used up new weavers' cottages with loom shops rose in every direction and filled with looms.[7]

The beneficial effects of the wealth-creating cotton industry, and the quickening of industry in general, are reflected in the development of Carlisle in the first two decades of the nineteenth century which will be examined before returning to the post-Napoleonic war problems of the textile industry and to the vicissitudes of the cotton weavers.

The 1805 map records the early stages of the factory age in the city. Two new cotton twist mills appear on the Corporation Dam south west of the Citadel, besides buildings, of an apparently industrial nature, opposite the Lamb Printfield, and a hat manufactory at the north end of George Street. Weaving, however, was still a cottage industry and the hand loom weaver was ubiquitous in Carlisle and the surrounding neighbourhood. Concentration of weavers appeared in Duke Street, Back Duke Street, Rigg Street and Caldcote in Caldewgate and Brown Street (south of the present Citadel Station).

The 1811 Jollie map shows major developments. The Citadel has been replaced by the Court Houses, Botchergate enters directly on to English Street and the old English Gate superseded. The Irish Gate went a few months later. In-filling was taking place in the town and the Lanes area now shows up as a high density development. Jollie comments

> . . . at the present day Carlisle in the openness of its principal streets, neatness and elegance of its buildings, and the decency and respectability of its inhabitants is excelled by few, if any, towns of equal size in Great Britain. Shops are numerous, many show a degree of taste and elegance, well furnished with every necessity of life, and not a few of its luxuries. Carlisle also affords several commodious Inns and maintains an intercourse with other parts of the island by several mail and stage coaches, wagons etc.[8]

A transformation indeed from the 1750 scene. A picture of Carlisle trade is given in the first edition of the *Carlisle Patriot*.

> Carlisle has now a population of 12,530. Over the past fifteen years the swing has been towards the manufacture of cotton goods; the greater part of which were ginghams for the West Indian market.[9]

Denton Holme to the west of the R. Caldew was becoming important industrially. A sale of land and premises belonging to Mr Dixon consisted of five industrial premises situated on the Mill Dam between Holme Head cotton twist mill and the Denton corn mills. The Denton Mill had two large water-wheels, carrying four pairs of stones for the grinding of corn and flour. Attached to the mill there was an indigo mill with a woollen manufactory and four loomed weaving shops. Then there was the Denton Holme print field,

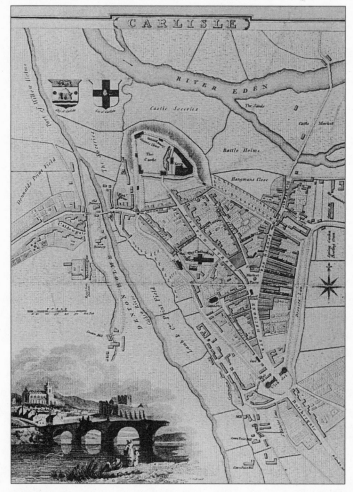

Roper and Brayley, 1805. A walled city with gardens and open spaces behind street frontage, but beginning of dense building in 'The Lanes'. Industrial development along Corporation Dam. Start of development outside city gates. R. Eden in two branches.

with printing shop, dye houses, drying house together with land for bleaching and drying (said to have been in operation for fifty years).[10]

By the second decade of the nineteenth century industrial development had profoundly altered the character of the city. The *Magna Britannica* of Lyson of 1816 delineates the industrial scene

A great change in the trade of Carlisle has taken place within the last fifteen years; it now consists almost entirely of the manufacture of cotton goods upon a very extensive scale. About 1,200 looms are employed in this manufacture in the town, and a still greater number in the neighbouring towns and villages. The principal articles made are ginghams for the West India markets. The spinning of cotton is carried on also to a considerable extent, there being 11 cotton-mills in the town and immediate vicinity, containing about 80,000 spindles. There are three print-works, where the printing of cotton is carried on very extensively, and various other concerns connected with the cotton trade, such as dying, bleaching, etc. A small mill for weaving calicoes, a manufactory of carpets, and three iron foundries, have been lately established; and there are four public breweries.[11]

The reference to the operation of power looms, at this early date for Carlisle, will assume greater importance when the poverty of hand loom weavers is discussed later in the chapter.

The city walls were by now a hindrance to an expanding city. The *Carlisle Journal* contended in 1803.

So long as the old walls remain standing the city can never properly extend itself. The population increases rapidly yet we can number no new streets; every little corner is built upon, to the great discomfort of the inhabitants, whereas if all obstructions were removed the town would rapidly extend itself.[12]

A major physical, and psychological, transformation of the Carlisle scene came with the final demolition of the city walls in 1813. The city had already extended into extra mural industrial areas but now the demolition symbolised a profound psychological change. The citizens were no longer part of an enclosed medieval community distrustful of, and on guard against, the outside world, they now accepted, and embraced enthusiastically, outside trade and contacts which were so necessary for the future of an industrial city. The demolition of the wall was followed by the building of the new Eden Bridge in 1814 with the former Priest Bech becoming the main channel of the Eden. The Scotch Gate was demolished and the stone used to fill part of the causeway between the two bridges.

Another civic amenity was now to be established, to the wonder of the citizens, which would make Carlisle both more agreeable and safer at night. In 1819 'An Act for lighting the City of Carlisle, and the suburbs thereof, with gas' was passed, and the Carlisle Gas, Light and Coke Company formed to supply the City with inflammable air or gas, and making and maintaining the works necessary for that purpose.[13] The Gas works were built at the junction of Collier Lane and the former Brown's Row.

The Wood map of 1821 shows new industrial development in the upper reaches of the Corporation Dam, a cotton twist mill of Mr Elliot (later Slaters) Cowan & Heysham cotton works, the Long Island cotton works and the newly erected bar-iron foundry of R. W. & R. Porter in Blackfriars Street. Carricks hat factory is now shown on Damside and Lowther Street is shown on the line of the former east curtain wall. Carlisle is no longer a fortified city of the Wood map. As today the west wall remains and two short sections of wall reach out from the Castle towards the town, but the rest of the city wall has gone.

The description of Carlisle by Lyson in 1816 is that of a city of thriving entrepreneurs, while the picture drawn by Jollie in 1811, of the more prestigious parts of the city, reflects an air of optimism. But the history of the ensuing decades do not justify the optimistic and complacent outlook.

The evidence is that while wealth was increasing rapidly in the early decades of the century, the poor were getting poorer and the contrast between the lives of the well heeled and those at the bottom end of the labour market, and we will be talking particularly of the ubiquitous hand loom weaver, was getting ever more dramatic and inevitably socially divisive. It can be maintained that an industrial revolution explicitly produces change and it is entirely plausible that industry would get out of balance and that social unfairness would result in the transition period, but the transition in the textile industry dragged out far longer than the word revolution would suggest. It has also been argued that the hand loom weaver in spite of increasing poverty was stubbornly clinging to a way of life and refusing to accept the regimentation and the constraints of a factory regime, but this argument loses much of its validity unless it can be shown that alternative employment was available to them. But these tentative judgements do not take into account the complexity of changes in early nineteenth century Carlisle. Other factors which come into play will be considered in some detail both because of their essential interest, and for their crucial influence in the occupation of great numbers of the Carlisle working class. The first of them was the explosive growth in the population of Carlisle in the first decades of the nineteenth Century, and the closely related factor of the massive immigration from Ireland and Scotland during that period. The immigration was on such a scale as to radically change the ethnic base of the population and regrettably the background of desperate poverty from which the immigrants were drawn inevitably led to debasement of living standards, and the erosion of wage rates in the city. The repercussions of this great influx of immigrants was an over abundant labour supply in the cotton industry, and it was the hand loom weavers who were the most vulnerable. The immense scale of the cottage industry in the early decades of the century, and the increasing deprivation of its workers, must be assessed quantitatively to be set against the optimistic picture drawn by Jollie. This must now be examined in some detail, concentrating first upon the demographic changes in Carlisle.

The burgeoning industrial growth in Carlisle in the early years of the nineteenth century led to a high, but unjustified, level of expectation which encouraged invasion by waves of immigrants from Ireland and Scotland. The initial step for the newcomer was deceptively easy, but the ultimate outcome was disastrous. A loom could be acquired for 1s a week rent and set up in the weaver's cottage, and the operation of a hand loom was a readily learnt skill. The new entrant to the trade was financially backed by the mill owner or master spinner, who with a plentiful supply of yarn, and an expanding market

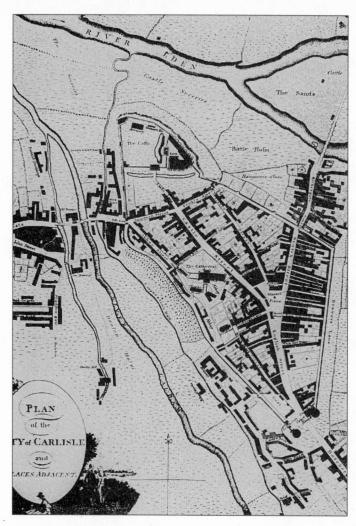

1811 – Jolie. Still a walled city but Citadel replaced by court houses. English gate replaced by direct entrance from Botchergate. Irish gate and Scotch gate and east city wall would disappear by 1813.

for cloth was ready to rent out a loom, supply yarn on credit, and to purchase the finished product, the woven cloth. The influx of immigrants caused an explosive growth in the population of Carlisle. For quinquennial periods between the year 1795 and 1820, whereas for the first period the population increased by 9%, the rate of increase had risen to 15% for the period 1815–1820. The greatest growth was in the new industrial areas outside the city walls, principally to the west and south of the city on the low lying areas along the R. Caldew and the Corporation Dam where the cotton industry took root and where the immigrants chiefly settled. Population statistics quoted by Dr Barnes[14] and summarised below, have been apportioned between the intra-mural areas of English Street, Scotch Street, Fisher Street, Castle Street and Abbey Street, and the extra-mural areas of Rickergate, Caldewgate and Botchergate.

1821 – Wood. No longer walled city. Heavy industrial development along Corporation Dam. Lowther Street appears on line of East Curtain Wall. City densely built up. Castle detached from city. Southern branch of Eden gone.

Growth in population of Carlisle 1788–1851

Year	1788	1801	1811	1821	1831	1841	1851
Intra-mural Area							
Population	4761	5745	6145	7199	8356	8456	8307
% Growth		20	7	17	16	2	−2
Extra-mural Area							
Population	2,555	3,882	5,467	7,362	10,713	13,227	18,039
% Growth		51	40	34	45	23	36

The settlement of weavers along the River Caldew was to become socially divisive. The new industrial area, physically separated from the town by the river and the high west walls, was accessible only at the north end by the old bridge across the Caldew, and remained so until the Nelson Bridge, built in the 1850s, joined the south end of the town and Botchergate, to the industrial area. In addition to the physical separation there was an economic and social barrier with the immigrants concentrated in the Caldew area, a poor, underprivileged and disenfranchised section of the population. When dire poverty was added to the other disabilities of the weaving community the seeds were sown for civic strife that at times made Caldewgate a 'no-go' area for police and magistrates.

The settlement of Irish and Scottish immigrants in the early nineteenth century changed radically the ethnic base of the Carlisle population. Available evidence suggests that immigrants from both countries entered Carlisle in comparable numbers. Dr Barnes quotes an entry in the *Carlisle Journal* of 1832 which asserted that of the 7,130 males over 20, 1,870 were born in Ireland and 1,000 in Scotland.[15] By the mid century the proportion had been reversed. In 1851 census returns for Carlisle record that 2,462 of the population had been born in Ireland and 3,271 in Scotland. (This would not include descendants of earlier generations of Scots and Irish, who had settled in Carlisle in the nineteenth century; the descendants while born in England, would have retained their ethnic roots and character). If the assumption is accepted that Irish and Scots did enter Carlisle in comparable numbers in the early decades of the nineteenth century; and, if an entry in the *Carlisle Journal* in 1827 reporting on unemployment in Carlisle, that 'for a population of 15,000 inhabitants one quarter of whom, perhaps, consist of poor Irish out of employment'[16] can be treated quantitatively, thus credence is given to Dr Barnes' suggestion 'that by the mid-1820s only half of the Carlisle population was Cumbrian born'.[17]

A more detailed examination of the 1851 census suggests that after 1830 the influx of immigrants tailed off sharply despite an expectation that the building of the railways in the 1840s would bring in an influx of 'navvies' from Ireland attracted by high wages. This conclusion is based upon an analysis of the census returns for the inhabitants of Carlisle District, who had been born in Cumberland, Scotland and Ireland for the age groups under 20 and 20 and over.

Carlisle and District Inhabitants 1851

Born in	Under 20	Over 20	Total
Cumberland	15,913	16,108	32,021
Ireland	643	1,819	2,462
Scotland	819	2,452	3,271
Total for all birth places:	18,545	23,014	

The low proportion of 'young' Scots and Irish in the Carlisle inhabitants in 1851, compared with the approximate equal numbers of 'young' and 'old' Cumbrians in Carlisle at that date, supports strongly the argument that there was not a heavy influx of immigrants from Scotland and Ireland into Carlisle in the period 1831–1851.

It was the misfortune of Carlisle that demographic forces were not only grossly out of step but also counter-productive to economic forces. The golden age for weavers was followed by a gross surplus of weavers after the Napoleonic wars, when foreign markets were lost after an indigenous cotton manufacturing industry was built up using yarn exported from Britain. Radcliffe campaigned hard for stopping surplus cotton yarn being exported because of the damage it would cause to English manufacturers. He had the threat of competition of low paid foreign weavers in mind when he wrote of

> hundreds of thousands of [Continental] weavers formerly employed in weaving linens, silks, stuffs etc., whose labour might be had at half the price such labour was paid for in this country.[18]

The excessive dependence of Carlisle on the weaving industry, and the consequent prospect of destitution of large sections of the population when the weaver came up against the hard economic fact of an overabundant labour supply in a competitive market, will be evident when the number employed in hand loom weaving in Carlisle is considered.

The attempt to assess the number of hand loom weavers in Carlisle in the first half of the nineteenth century is rendered difficult because of the ambiguity in the evidence available. There were as many weavers in the surrounding district as in the city itself and the distinction between city, and Carlisle district is not always clearly made. Again, while weaving was a whole family occupation, a distinction has to be made between the numbers of people dependent upon weaving, i.e. the weaver himself and those, perhaps children, assisting in the preparation. It is also necessary to differentiate between the weaver employed by Carlisle manufacturers and Carlisle weavers when according to the evidence in the muggeridge Report of 1840, Peter Dixon & Sons of Carlisle 'employed 3,571 hand loom weavers, namely 2,389 in England, 599 in Scotland and 583 in Ireland.'[19] Contrariwise there is evidence that in the 1860s weavers in Carlisle were not entirely employed by the big Carlisle firms, such as Dixons, but also by Glasgow firms.[20]

The assessment of the extent of hand loom weaving in Carlisle made below is, because of the consistency of the information, based upon the number of looms employed in the city. From these figures it is possible, to make a reasonable assessment of the numbers actively employed in hand weaving, and the number of those dependent upon weaving, from the detailed enumeration of Carlisle weavers, and their families, contained in the Muggeridge Report.

Muggeridge, in his 1840 Report on Hand loom weavers says that a survey in Carlisle 'was drawn up with great care' and gave the following results:[21]

Number of looms	1963
Number of families	994
Number of persons	3814
Number of children	2188
of whom — were weaving	813
— employed by other businesses	172
— unemployed	1203

from which it can simply be calculated that 18% of the total Carlisle population of 21,200 in 1840 was dependent upon hand loom weaving. The upper limit for those actively employed in weaving, adults and children who weave, was 2,439 [i.e. 3,814, 2,188 + 813], i.e. 64% of the family; and that the ratio of active weavers to looms = 1.24

The looms employed in Carlisle at various times were:

> 1816 1,200 looms in Carlisle, with another 1,000 in surrounding villages.[22]
> 1840 1,963 looms. Muggeridge.
> 1846 1,600 looms.[23]

There are other estimates of the number of weavers in Carlisle which would appear to give much higher figures than above. Dr Barnes quotes from a *Carlisle Journal* reference of 1825 which states that there were 5,000 weavers in Carlisle at that time,[24] but this high figure would suggest that it referred to the district, rather than the city.

The number of hand loom weavers in Carlisle appeared to have peaked probably before 1840 and there was a substantial decline by 1846, but even in the 1860s many Carlisle hand loom weavers were trying to eke out a living on their antiquated machines. James Walter Brown reminiscing of the 1860s said

> Hand-loom weaving was still engaged in, this being an important part of Messrs Dixon's business, which had found employment for some thousands of hands in Carlisle and throughout the Border Counties. Whole streets were filled with hand looms, but the trade was then decaying . . .[25]

While Mr J. Couch's recollections of the 1870s were 'what a nest of hand-loom weaving was Duke Street – back and front – Broadguards, Rigg Street and Queen Street' in Shaddongate.[26]

The great influx of immigrants to Carlisle and the consequent overmanning of the hand loom weaving industry inevitably had repercussions on the wages and wellbeing of the weavers in a laissez faire economic system in which market forces were blind to the basic needs of the deprived worker or to the requirements of a socially cohesive society. Following the invention of spinning machinery, and the subsequent abundant supply of yarn for his loom, the weaver's earning rocketed to a level of prosperity which he could hardly have imagined before, and yet within a quarter of a century, largely due to an over-abundance of labour, he was reduced to dire poverty. The rise of the weaver's earnings form 1770, at the start of the industrial revolution in textiles, to the boom years of the cottage weaver at the beginning of the nineteenth century was meteoric. In 1770 Radcliffe asserted the father of a family would earn from 8s to 10/6d at his loom, and his sons, if he had one, two or three alongside him, 6s or 8s each per week.[27] The effect of the more abundant supply of yarn of the cottager and his family was, initially equivocal; while the income of the weaver was boosted this was counterbalanced by the decreased demand for work from the spinning wheel. Eden records an increase in income for the Carlisle weaver in the 1790s. 'A good weaver, with constant work, can earn 12s to 15s a week, but in general 8s or 9s a week seem to be the usual earnings'.[28] With the introduction of the Mule at the end of the century the weaver reached the zenith of his prosperity. The average earnings for the hand loom weaver are recorded annually for the period of prosperity c. 1800 and for the subsequent four decades of decline,[29] and the wages have been related to the price of the weaver's basic food and rent[30] in Table No. 1.

Table No. 1: Average Wage (shillings and pence) for hand loom weavers

Year	Weekly Wage	7 Year Period	Average over seven years		
			Average Wage	Food in lbs	Rent Index
1797	29				
1798	30				
1799–1801	25	1797–1804	26/8d	281	6
1802	29				
1803–4	24				
1805	25				
1806	22				
1807	18	1804–1811	20/-	238	9
1808	15				
1809	16				
1810	19/6d				
1811–12	14				
1813	15				
1814	24				
1815	14	1811–1818	14/2d	131	12½
1816	12				
1817–18	9				
1819–20	9/6d	1818–1825	8/9d	108	16
1821–25	8/6d				
1826	7				
1827	6/6d	1825–1832	6/4d	83	22
1828	6				
1829–36	5/6d	1832–1834	5/6d	83	25
1837	4/6d				
1838	5/6d				

The table should be interpreted thus: from 1797 to 1804 a weaver could earn 26/8d per week which would buy him 100lbs of flour, or 142lbs of oatmeal or 826lbs of potatoes, or 55lbs of butcher's meat; which would give general average of relative proportions of these articles of 281lbs.[31]

The rent index shows the relative amount of work that a weaver has to perform to meet his rent. Thus 6 pieces of woven cloth would be required in the period 1797–1804, but for the last period 1832–1834 he would need to weave 25 pieces.

The figure represent net wage, after a deduction of 27½% for loom rent, winding, oil and candles for the shop.

The average earnings on a piece rate system conceal however, great variations depending on the capability of the weaver, whether he was experienced or an untrained newcomer, adult or adolescent, full time or on part time when demand was low. Evidence given in the Muggeridge Report of 1,840 shows a wide range of earnings. When the average earnings in Carlisle was 4/6d net per week, some families, with teenage children, earned considerably more. Mr George Dixon, giving evidence to the Muggeridge Committee, selected the earnings of 'those of our best and most regular workmen and who are employed generally on our best fabrics.'[32]

Handcock Long			George Coulthard			Joseph Hind			James Davidson		
	s	d		s	d		s	d		s	d
Self	8	4	Self	5	6	Self	7	2	Self	5	6
Son	5	8	Son	4	5	Wife	4	9	Son	5	7
Son	5	10	Son	4	2	Son	3	9	Dgtr	5	5
Son	4	6				Dgtr	4	7	Dgtr	5	5
	24	4		13	11		20	3		21	11

After the boom year of 1805, the earnings settled down to a somewhat reduced, but still high, level to the end of the Napoleonic Wars. This brought to an end the considerable war time market for the products of the textile industry, but hopes must have been high that the opening up of the continent for trade, and the revival of trade with America, would bring a great expansion of trade for the industry. But it was not the weavers that were going to prosper, the export of the great quantities of yarn that were now available enabled foreign weavers to expand their production to supply their own markets. The effect was to reduce the demand for the products of the English hand loom weaver and drastically weaken his position vis a vis his employer, the master weaver and manufacturer.

Two major factors in the post war years caused a severe depression of wages in the period up to 1825, and thereafter a calamitous drop to a sub-subsistence wage. The first factor was the overabundance of labour in the weaving industry; the second was the use of social expediences that, whatever was the intention, effectively pauperised the weaver.

Evidence has already been given of the great inflow of immigrants into Carlisle from Ireland and Scotland in the early decades of the nineteenth century and clearly the livelihood of the weaver was seriously threatened when large numbers of families took up the trade in the absence of effective regulation by unions or guild, and in a political climate where governmental interference in industry was looked upon as an affront to laissez faire. The response of the Parliamentary Committee appointed to examine the petition of Lancashire cotton workers, who sought to relieve their distress by proposing to fix a minimum price of labour, and to limit the number of apprentices, was negative and uncompromising.

That the Prepositions stated in the said Petitions relative to the fixing of a Minimum for the Price of labour in the cotton manufacture is wholly inadmissible in principle, incapable of being reduced in practice by any means which can possibly be devised, and if practicable would be productive of the most fatal consequences: That the Preposition relative to the limiting the number of Apprentices is also entirely inadmissible, and would, if adopted by the House be attended with the greatest injustice to the manufacturer, as well as the labourer.[33]

By 1830 however authoritative people were recognising how pernicious these principles were. Muggeridge in the Report stated his judgement why the state of the weavers was so deplorable. He wrote:

(i) The disproportionate number of weavers to the labour required to be performed by them.
(ii) The fact of a knowledge of the weaving trade being easily acquired, and of the trade itself being open to all classes of unemployed persons.

The Report continued:

In the recollection of almost all the old weavers, it was stated, that the practice of apprenticeship to the loom was general, and that at such periods, the labour of the weaver had been adequately requited; but vast numbers of destitute persons had entered the trade, which, with agricultural labour, were the only refuges, and became one of the main causes of the reduction which had taken place in the wages of weaving.[34]

An unrestricted entry to the trade was obviously to the disadvantage of the weavers, but some of the manufacturers also were not happy about the results this produced. Thus William Harling, a manufacturer, stated in his evidence to the Committee:

In less than 12 months inexperienced men will draw out work as weavers; they will not be good or efficient workmen in that time; their work will be badly done, and such men are a constant drag on the trade. These are the sort of men that will work at the lowest rate of wages, or at any rate offered, and spoil the work when they have got it. A legislative enactment, compelling men to serve as apprentices, would be advantageous.[35]

The second factor that was to pauperise the weavers in their desperate situation was the pernicious social practice for poor relief first introduced in 1795. Under the Speenhamland system wages were supplemented out of the poor rate when these were considered to be too low relative to the price of bread and the size of the recipient's family. This system not only hit the rate-payer hard, but it pauperised many of the low paid workers and destroyed their bargaining power as masters took advantage of the legislation, and in the highly competitive post-war markets the wages of the weavers were reduced to a sub-subsistence level.

The baneful effects of the system spread wider. The competition of subsidized labour inevitably threatened the wage level in areas where the susidy was not paid.

It can be argued that the average wages given in Table No. 1 are not a true reflection of the operation of a laissez faire economic system. In the post-war years wages descended to a sub-subsistence level that could not have been viable in a free economic system. It was ironically an interference with the system, by subsidising wages out of the poor rate, that permitted the wage rate of drop to such an abysmal level. It is to support this contention that a brief review will be made of poverty in Carlisle in the first two decades of the century, before it will be noted, the widespread introduction of the power loom. In 1812 the *Carlisle Journal* reported, 1,081 families were being relieved by public subscription; the majority were said to have been those of weavers.[36] This gives an astonishing 39% of the population receiving some form of relief.

In 1817 complaints were voiced of the hordes of newcomers coming to the city asking for poor relief. The Overseer or St Mary's parish complained to the local MP's that

Numerous hordes of the idle and unsettled . . . were arriving in Carlisle with the fixed idea that the authorities are obliged to maintain and support them.[37]

Which suggests that many over sanguine immigrants never really got started in the industry.

An estimate was made in the *Carlisle Journal* in 1819 of the poor and very poor, living in Carlisle at this time. It asserted that:

⅛ of the population consists of paupers living on the contribution of the rest.

⅜'s have low wages and live on a pittance.

¼ with difficulty support their families.

⅛ – the middle class – struggle to maintain their place in society.

⅛ – are exempt from this disorganised state of existence.[38]

It is evident that one half of the population of the city lived in dire poverty and another quarter only survived with difficulty.

Two supposedly major influences on wage rates have still to be considered, but their actual effect on average wages shown in the table, is surprisingly small. The first influence was the introduction of the power loom into factories and loom shops; the second, the legislation of the Poor Law Amendment Act of 1834 which purported to end the Speenhamland system, thus to reduce the poor rate and to permit wages to rise to their true market level.

Cartwright's improved power loom was invented in 1785, but its development was initially unsuccessful. Further premature attempts were made but it was not until the period 1803–1813 that patents were taken out for improved machines that overcame the severe operational problems of the earlier models. In contrast to its later reluctance to accept the new technology, Carlisle was to the fore in pioneering the new invention. Jollie wrote in 1811:

> At Long Island, Messrs Holme have their manufactory for weaving, which is performed by the cast iron looms, that go by steam, and which they have the credit of introducing into this part.[39]

In addition early models of the power loom were manufactured in Carlisle. Jollie stated 'On Damside [there is] the workshop of Mr Marsden, a very ingenious manufacturer of the steam looms.'[40]

The use of power looms, in England and Scotland expanded very rapidly within a period of two decades as the table, based on the Muggeridge Report[41] clearly shows

Power looms in use

Year	England	Scotland
1813	2,400	
1820	12,150	2,000
1829	45,500	10,000
1833	85,000	15,000
1835	97,564	17,721

The potential threat of the power loom, to the living of the hand loom weaver is apparent in the evidence, submitted to the Muggeridge Committee by a

Lancastrian manufacturer, on the comparative outputs of the power and hand looms.[42]

Date	Method	Pieces per Week	Looms	Operatives
1840	Good hand loom weaver	2	1	1 aged 25–30
1823	Steam loom weaver	7	2	1 boy aged 15
1826	Steam loom weaver	12–15	2	1 boy aged 15

The power loom gave an increase in productivity of at least 6 times, with financial advantage to the operator notwithstanding a lower rate per piece of cloth. The Report stated that 'although the piece rate for the power loom weaver is one third that of the hand loom weaver, the earnings of the former are greater than that of the latter.'[43]

In spite of the advantage to manufacturer, and operator, the widespread adoption of the power loom in Carlisle was surprisingly late. In 1829 only 89 power looms were employed in Carlisle out of a total of 45,000 in England,[44] but the evidence is that in the next 10 years Carlisle had followed the national trend.

Table No. 1 can be studied to find the effect of the introduction of power looms on the wages of the hand loom weaver. The drop in wages from 1825 can be correlated with the increased use of power looms, but by 1829 the wage rate had stabilised and was not further influenced by the great expansion in the use of power looms from that date.

One can surmise that wages were by then sub-subsistence and could not well have been reduced further without an outcry by the rate payers. The laissez faire economic system had been so distorted by the Speenhamland system that wage rates no longer represented what it cost to live.

The Poor Law Amendment Act of 1834 set out to abolish the Speenhamland system. 'Men must be discouraged from becoming paupers and outdoor relief must be strongly discouraged.' Parishes were grouped into Unions and workhouses set up.[45] The regime was designed to be so harsh that only the genuine destitute would allow themselves to become a burden on the parish. Pringle defined the purpose of the workhouse:

A poor-house should combine the uses of a hospital with that of a place of restraint to the idle and dissipated. Classification should be a primary consideration, particularly separating from the adults the children, who might then be expected to turn out as well as those of their own class in ordinary life. The inform, the aged and the young, are then legitimate objects and for their reception such an establishment will always be required. Those able to work should be induced by restraint, and the fair proportion of work exacted from them, to endeavour to find means of supporting themselves. Separation of sexes should be enforced, even with married couples who throw themselves on parish relief, making them understand that they are not to add pauper children to the population, to be supported at the expense of the good conduct and industrious habits of the others.[46]

The splitting of families was not confined to the workhouse; the family of a recipient on out-relief could also be split up. A clause in Pringle's Report states:

The giving relief, according to a scale regulated by the number of children, should certainly be prohibited; and on any one claiming relief, from inability to maintain above a certain number, the others should be received into the poor-house.[47]

The Poor Law Amendment Act did not terminate out door relief to the able bodied poor if it was expedient to continue with the old system, in spite of its professed intention, nor did it persuade manufacturers to increase wages to the hand loom weaver as is evident by referring to the Table No. 1 for the years 1834 to 1838, on the contrary the average wage for the year 1837 dropped to 4/6d per week. The weaver was still pauperised and only able to survive by submitting to a harsh and humiliating means test.

The numbers of people on out-relief in Carlisle was, as the Report said 'very considerable'. There were 258 people receiving regular pensions, 258 receiving casual relief throughout the year, but double that number during the winter months. To this must be added 183 paupers in the work house, and 80 illegitimate children; equivalent to a total of 865 throughout the year[48] which amounted to one pauper in 23 in a Carlisle population of 20,000.[49]

The City Council appointed a Mendicity Society in January 1842 to enquire into the state of the poor in Carlisle and to devise means for their temporary relief. A summary of their findings is given in Table No. 2. The figures show that 309 families, comprising 1,146 individuals, were completely destitute and relied entirely upon public charity. In all 1,351 families of 5,561 people, that is one quarter of the inhabitants, were living on 3s. per person per week, or less, with the greatest concentration of the poor in the Caldewgate and Botchergate districts.

The deprivation of the hand loom weaver has been depicted mainly in statistical terms. It remains to describe the conditions of the Carlisle weaver in terms connected with everyday life.

On what do these people live. Oatmeal gruel form their breakfast; potatoes with dripping or the liquid fat from a little morsel of bacon, their dinner; and either a drink of beer (so small that it is sold at a penny a gallon!) or a mere drink called 'tea' is taken with bread as the evening meal. Butcher's meat, many of these men and their families do not taste often for six, nine or twelve months together. As to clothing, a hand-loom weaver, after

The state of the poor in Carlisle 1841

District	Families with no settled income		Families receiving less than 1s. per head per week		Families receiving less than 1s. 6d. per head per week		Families receiving less than 2s. per head per week		Families receiving less than 3s. per head per week		Total number of	
	Families	Persons	Families	Persons	Families	Persons	Families	Persons	Families	Persons	Families	Persons
Caldewgate	88	326	108	479	226	914	34	141	56	314	512	2174
St Cuthberts	25	98	40	194	45	226	56	274	58	223	224	1017
St Marys	5	10	20	60	27	65	5	20	6	25	63	180
Botchergate	133	506	120	570	61	242	36	127	20	73	370	1518
Rickergate	58	206	46	162	52	174	26	130	—	—	182	672
Total	309	1146	334	1465	411	1625	157	692	140	635	1351	5561

Source: Carlisle Journal 1 January 1842
The total population in Carlisle 1842 was approximately 22,000.

marriage, scarcely expects to purchase a new coat; he may be able to obtain a second hand one from a pawn shop, stores are usually to be had that have remained past the legal time of redemption, but a patched up covering he has had for years is usually all his change for a Sunday . . . he saunters in the lanes or into the fields, rather than show his tatters and threadbare habit in a church or chapel. The loom shops, which usually hold 4 looms, and less frequently, but two, are wretched places. For avoiding dryness that would injure their work, they are sunk below the level of the street, and are unpaved either with brick or stone. I shall never forget my visit to one of these squalid cells where the family lived. A father with his daughter and 2 boys were working in it – but this man has taken a room overhead, as a sleeping place for the whole family. His daughter's average earnings were 4s. weekly, the elder boy's 2s. and the younger boy's 1s 6d; for having to attend to his children's work, he could not earn more than 6s. himself. Thus a man, his wife, his daughter, 2 boys and an infant had thus to be supported on 13s 6d a week. The weaver's house – or rather room – for he has often but one for himself and family has to be rented.[50]

NOTES

1. Andrew Ure, *The Philosophy of Manufacturers* (1835).
2. Anon., *The Poor Cotton Weaver*, early nineteenth-century ballad.
3. William Radcliffe was a Lancastrian cotton spinner and merchant and a prominent writer on the early history of the cotton industry.
4. William Radcliffe, *Origin of the New System of Manufacturing Commonly Called Power-loom Weaving* (1828). Reprinted 1974. pp. 59–60.
5. See Appendix No. 2 for Technology of Cotton Industry,
6. Radcliffe, op. cit., p. 49.
7. Radcliffe, op. cit., p. 65.
8. Jollie Directory (1811), p. 9.
9. *Carlisle Patriot*, 5 June 1815.
10. *Carlisle Journal*, 1 May 1819.
11. Lyson, *Magna Britannic vol.4 Cumberland* (1816), p. 6.
12. *Carlisle Journal*, 8 October 1803. Quoted from Dr June Barnes, *Popular Protest and Radical Politics 1790–1850* (1981), pp. 24–5.
13. 59 Geo. III c4.
14. J. Barnes, op. cit., p. 25.
15. J. Barnes, op. cit., p. 40. Quote from *Carlisle Journal*, 3 May 1832.
16. *Carlisle Journal*, 20 January 1827.
17. J. Barnes, op. cit., p. 38.
18. Radcliffe, op. cit., p. 49.
19. R. M. Muggeridge. *Report on Condition of Hand-loom Weavers of Counties of Lancaster, Westmorland, Cumberland and Part of the West Riding of Yorkshire*, pp 1840, xxiv, p. 586.
20. *Carlisle Journal*, 28 April 1933. Letter from Mr J. Couch.

21. Muggeridge, op. cit., p. 584.
22. Lyson, op. cit., p. 6.
23. Douglas Jerrold's Weekly Newspaper, October 1846.
24. J. Barnes, op. cit., pp. 23–4.
25. James Walter Brown, *Round Carlisle Cross*, 'Carlisle Seventy Years Ago', ii, p. 39.
26. *Carlisle Journal*, 28 April 1933. Letter from Mr J. Couch.
27. Radcliffe, op. cit., p. 59.
28. F. M. Eden, *The State of the Poor* (1797; re-issued 1966), p. 60.
29. Muggeridge PP (1840), xxiv, p. 392.
30. PP (1835), vol. xiii, Report from Select Committee on hand loom weavers, p. 341.
31. The average weekly wages are taken from the Muggeridge Report p. 592. An estimate of what these wages would command in terms of weight of food in a representative 'shopping basket', and the 'rent index', are contained in the Select Committee's Report on Hand-Loom Weavers, p. xiii, but the Report does not specify the composition of this 'shopping basket'. From the figures it is evident that there was a catastrophic fall in the wage rate for hand loom weavers from 1797 to 1838. This was partly, but by no means adequately, compensated by a fall in food prices. Thus in 1838 the wage rate was a mere 19% of its value in 1797 but the corresponding weight of the 'shopping basket' was 30% of its former value.
32. Muggeridge, op. cit., pp. 586–7.
33. PP 1808, *Report on the Petition of Several Weavers*, vol. III, p. 111.
34. Muggeridge, op. cit., p. 604.
35. Ibid.
36. *Carlisle Journal*, 12 June 1812.
37. *Carlisle Journal*, 28 February 1817.
38. J. Barnes, op. cit., p. 18. Quotation from *Carlisle Journal*, 3 March 1819.
39. Jollie, op. cit., p. 83.
40. Ibid.
41. Muggeridge, op. cit., p. 591.
42. Ibid.
43. Muggeridge, op. cit., p. 590.
44. Bouch and Jones, *Short Economic and Social History of the Lake Counties*, p. 268.
45. Mannix and Whellan, op. cit., p. 137. Three Carlisle Workhouses were named. St Mary's, near Irishgate brow (1785). St Cuthberts at Harraby Hill (1809) and Caldewgate at Coal-fell Hill (1829–30), but all three had been set up before the Poor Law Amendment Act of 1834 was passed, and no new ones were built for the Union. The Caldewgate work house was, however, subsequently enlarged so as to accommodate 130 paupers. For the quarter ending June 1846 there were 2,194 paupers in the Carlisle Union work houses, 1,774 outdoor and 420 indoor.
46. Captain Pringle, *The Commissioners of the Poor Laws Report* Appendix A.P.P. (1834), XVIII, p. 329A.
47. Pringle, op. cit., p. 327A.
48. In this calculation the additional 258 people receiving relief for the 4 winter months are equivalent to $\frac{1}{3}$ of that number for a complete year.
49. Pringle op. cit. p. 322A.
50. *Douglas Jerrold's Weekly Newspaper* October 1846.

CHAPTER 4

The Urban Scene. Nineteenth-Century Carlisle. A Dark Chapter

Dirty habits . . . do no great harm in the countryside where the population is scattered. On the other hand, the dangerous situation which develops when such habits are practised among the crowded populations of big cities, must arouse feelings of apprehension and disgust.

F. Engels[1]

Earlier chapters have borne witness to the growth of Carlisle and its industries and to the vastly improved communications that linked the city to the nation and to the world at large, but cognizance has been taken of a dangerously unbalanced society, and a cautionary word has been written of the dangers inherent in a society with a large section of the citizens in a state of extreme poverty. Now a dark chapter must be written on the crudities and dangers of the nineteenth century urban living conditions. This can be done in great detail. The nineteenth century was a period when the body and soul of the city, the actual living conditions and attitudes of the urban population, was opened to view to a degree unprecedented in the nation's history. The body of the city, in the most intimate detail, was exposed to public inspection by skilled and clinical interrogation. The soul of the city, with its ambivalent attitude to whether the rewards of the machine age were to serve man or mammon, was opened up for the judgement of contemporaries, or for inquisitive posterity.

The late eighteenth century, and the first half of the nineteenth century witnessed an explosive growth in the population of Carlisle, which was to have a profound effect on the quality of life of its citizens. The effect of this growth will be studied in some detail. Roper and Brayley 1805 map shows a city spilling out of the confines of its medieval walls at its three gates, Botchergate, Rickergate and Caldewgate, and along the 'Dam' outside the west wall of the city. The census compiled by Dr Heysham in 1779, which enumerated separately the number of inhabitants in the intra-mural city; the extra-mural areas outside the three city gates; and in the nearby villages, provides a valuable guide to the relative quality of housing in different parts of the city. The table below is a summary of the population statistics for the three main areas.[2]

1. Within the medieval walls.

2. Extra-mural areas adjacent to 'Botchard Gate', 'Richard Gate' and 'Caldew Gate'.

3. Nearby villages. viz. 'New-Town', Harraby, Carleton, Wreay, Brisco, 'Botchardby', 'Uprightby', 'Black-hill', Cummersdale, Moreton-Head and Newby.

		1779				1787
	Inhabitants	Houses	Families	Families per House	Inhabitants per House	Inhabitants
1. Within the walls	3,504	549	870	1.58	6.38	4,805
2. Without the walls	2,795	342	735	2.15	8.17	2,555
3. Villages	1,378	257	267	1.03	5.36	1,317
	7,677	1,148	1,872			8,677

By 1779 the 'without the walls' area, low lying and becoming increasingly small scale industrial, was already a low grade housing area with severe over-crowding. Surprisingly the conditions in the supposedly confined intra mural area were more tolerable with, apart form the 'Lanes' area, gardens behind the main city streets. The villages, whether the houses were hovels or not, were relatively spacious. The city grew rapidly during the 1780s and by 1787 the population density 'within the walls' had increased by 37% and the problem areas, as regards health hazards, were developing.

In the early nineteenth century it was the extra mural areas of the city that experienced the most rapid growth. Rawlinson's analysis of the census returns of 1841,[3] cognizance is taken of the demolition of the city walls in 1813, St Mary's and St Cuthbert's constitute the inner city. Rickergate, Caldewgate and 'St Cuthbert's without' correspond to the Heysham 'without the walls' area.

	'Within the Walls'	'Without the Walls'	Villages	Total
1787	4,805	2,555	1,317	8,677
1841	8,356	13,496	2,081	23,933
% Increase	74	428	56	176

A half century of population growth resulted in a massive 428% increase in the outer industrial areas, particularly Caldewgate and Botchergate, but there was also a very significant increase in population density in the 'inner city'.[4] Rawlinson reported in 1850:

A great portion of the present crowded state of the buildings in the centre of the city is comparatively modern. Most of the confined lanes, yards, courts and alleys were, in the first instance, gardens attached to houses, fronting the main streets. These houses have gradually been changed from private dwellings into shops, hotels, taverns, stables, workshops, offices and outhouses, until every available open space has now been built upon.[5]

From this demographic perspective of the Carlisle scene in the first half of the nineteenth century it now remains to focus for a closer look at urban housing and living conditions. The documentation to be called upon is chiefly that of the Second Report of the Royal Commission of 1845, with its invaluable Appendix 2 in which Dr Reid reports on Carlisle in particular,[6] and Rawlinson's Report to the General Board of Health on the City of Carlisle' of 1850.[7] The reader is also referred to Sir John Walsham's Report of 1840[8] and Edwin Chadwick's Report of 1842.[9]

This close up view will authenticate the assertions made of the absence of basic housing amenities, primitive water supply, sewerage, and scavenging services, in as much details may be required, and open up to public inspection the degradation of the lives of large sections of the citizens caused by unregulated urban growth. A recurrent underlying theme will be the resigned acquiescence of local government to the squalid living conditions to which large sections of the deprived population seem to have become inured. However much those in positions of power and authority might avert their eyes from an unpleasant picture[10] the facts of the situation had been precisely and objectively reported.

Firstly the general scene, c. 1850, will be portrayed in the words of Rawlinson.

The working classes of Carlisle live almost entirely in lanes, between the principal and secondary streets . . . it is asserted that from 9 to 10 thousand persons reside in these lanes, courts and alleys . . . Many of these lanes are entered by a covered passage and some are closed at one end. They are in general only a few yards in width. In some the doors are opposite each other and not more than 3 yards apart . . . in many instances there is only one privy to a whole lane and these ruinous and filthy. In some lanes privies and middens are crowded among the houses and not infrequently under the same roof. They are in contact with a dwelling house on each side and have living and sleeping rooms above them. The infiltration from the middens and liquid refuse in contact with the wall, in some instances passes through, to the great inconvenience of the adjoining occupants. Some of the cottages are built back to back when in a single row they have all the faults of a double structure in not having windows, or ventilation openings, in the back or side walls. The houses are let off in tenancies having one common stair to several tenancies.[11]

Rawlinson now focused more finely on the housing in two particular localities for which plans were available in the Reid Report of 1845. The plans bring home to the reader, even more than the printed word, the conditions under which the poor were housed.

Plan No. 1 shows congested slum property in the city in the mid nineteenth century and not serviced by sewers in 1850. An appalling conglomeration of dwelling houses, shops, pig sties, stables and ash pits. A close inspection of the plan will reveal the horrors of mid century slums.[12]

Plan No. 2 shows the 'Lanes' area. Rawlinson reports:

> This block of property consists of lanes, courts, out-yards, banks, shops, hotels, stables and cow sheds, schools and dwelling houses, amongst which are crowded and confined yards, privies, cess pools, middens and other nuisances. Many of the privies and cess pools are in immediate contact with the dwelling houses. Some are within them, the cess pools and middens extending beneath the living or sleeping-room floor. Drainage is either absent or most imperfect, surface channels alone having been provided, not however with any view to refuse drainage, for this purpose they ought not to be used, but merely to carry away rainfall.[13]

Rawlinson's deplored this state of affairs, with lack of house ventilation. He maintained 'no fact is more firmly established than the one which places foul air and excess of epidemic, endemic and contagious diseases, as cause and effect'. The dangers of these conditions to public health remain unchallenged but this miasmic theory was superseded by the germ theory in medical circles in the latter part of the century. The relationship between foul air and bad smells, and epidemic and endemic diseases is now viewed as contingent rather than causal.

'The Lanes' as referred to in this history will readily be remembered but sanitised by Carlisle citizens of 1980s but may cause difficulties for future generations. This area, after years of agonizing by city authorities has been cleared and rebuilt as a new shopping complex. The layout of the new development bears only vestigial resemblance to the 'old lanes' but fortunately the inappropritess of block building has been avoided and the facades of the new buildings are not out of sympathy with the present city centre.

The squalor of the inner city was, on the evidence of the Rawlinson report, exceeded by the sanitary horrors in the low lying industrial areas outside the city gates. Some examples, out of the numerous cases in the Report, can be quoted to give an indication of the magnitude of the health hazard and the sheer degradation of the lives of the urban poor. Attention was drawn to Strong's-buildings, situated in Bridge Street (Caldewgate), and Willowholme, where most intolerable nuisances exist – damp miserable cellars, and dwellings above and on each side of most fearful dirty privies. Everything in this range of buildings, containing more than 200 people, betokens the greatest filth and

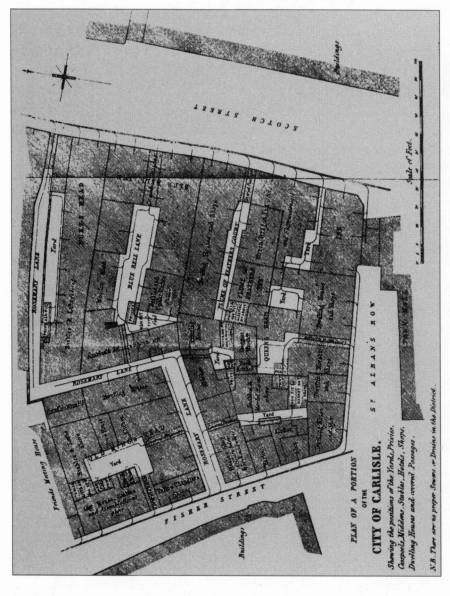

PLAN OF A PORTION
OF THE
CITY OF CARLISLE,

*Shewing the positions of the Yards, Privies,
Cesspools, Middens, Stables, Hotels, Shops,
Dwelling Houses and covered Passages.*

N.B. There are no proper Sewers or Drains in the District.

The urban scene: urban squalor persisted into the 20th century. (Cumbria Record Office)

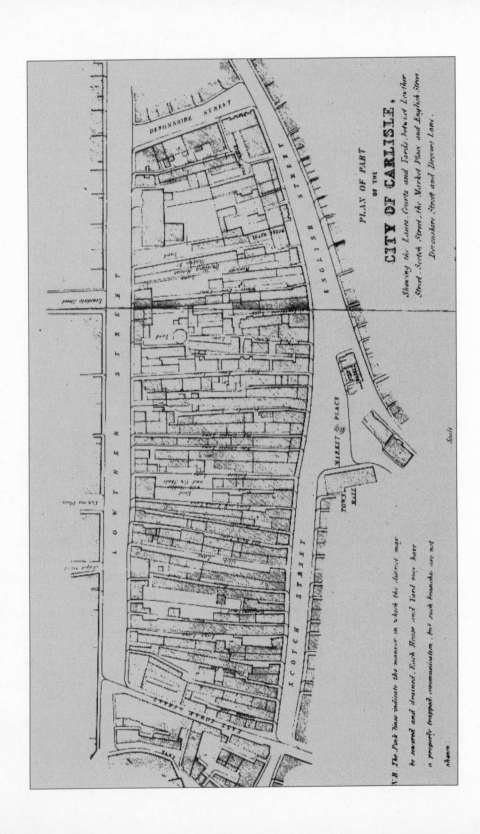

PLAN OF PART
OF THE
CITY OF CARLISLE,

Showing the Lanes, Courts and Yards between Lowther
Street, Scotch Street, the Market Place and English Street,
Devonshire Street and Devons Lane.

N.B. The Dark lines indicate the manner in which the district may
be covered and drained. Each House and Yard may have
a properly trapped communication, but such branches are not
shewn.

Scale

physical deprivation; and here fever committed sad ravages during last autumn'.[14] Other examples in Caldewgate are cited. 'In Church Street the large open drain is very offensive.' 'In Bridge Street the lanes are in a deplorable state of filth; in one of these eight pig sties, cowhouses, and large pools of stagnant noxious fluid.' 'In Brewery row there was only one privy for 20 families, and this has not been cleaned out since built.'[15]

It is tempting to postulate that the extent of the abysmal housing in Carlisle thus described would correspond closely with the proportion of the population living on a bare subsistence wage or charity. The supposition is supported convincingly by comparing Rawlinson's estimate of 9 to 10 thousand living in lanes, courts, alleys', in 1850, i.e. up to 40% of the population with an estimate made in the *Carlisle Journal* of the poor living in Carlisle in 1819,[16] if one makes allowance for a limited economic improvement by the mid century. The Journal's estimate which was given in the previous Chapter showed that at least half of Carlisle's population could be classed as destitute, or very poor, with little or no choice of abode, while an additional quarter led a precarious existence and by necessity would have to be very tolerant of the living conditions that they could be prepared to accept. Only the upper quartile would have a reasonable choice in their living conditions.

It is evident from contemporary records that there were degrees of 'extreme poverty' in an impoverished community. Two sections of the community will be singled out, the hand loom weavers, and the lowest class of all, the people of no fixed abode, the tramps and vagrants who resided, for varying periods, in the town's lodging houses. Both groups, because of their destitution and squalid living conditions, were a serious health hazard, to themselves, and to the community at large.

Dr Reid comments on the condition of the hand loom weavers:

> The hand loom weavers are a numerous body, who have for many years worked for very low wages, their sedentary and constant occupation renders them liable to take disease more readily than those more actively employed, but it is probable that this class are still more subject to disease from deficient food, and being crowded together in ill ventilated dwellings; they form a large proportion of the patients of the medical charities.[17]

The crowded living conditions of the weavers were aggravated, in many cases, by the necessity of erecting the loom in the dwelling room. Reid cites Brown's Row,[18] where there were descriptions of rooms met with in this place (and common to several other places, viz. Broadguards, Duke-street, Water-street etc. of very small bedrooms, partitioned from the general apartments only sufficiently large to take two beds, with a small space of from one foot and a half to two feet between them; when the door is closed, and these beds occupied by 5 or 6 individuals, the atmosphere must be almost suffocating.[19]

Globe Lane, demolished in The Lanes development in 1984. (*Carlisle Archaeological Unit*)

Undoubtedly, however, the worst housing conditions in the city were in the common lodging houses, stages for the tramps and mendicants who travelled the country from end to end, and who were one of the chief agents for the spread of disease. Rawlinson tells us that there were '360 men, women and children sleeping habitually within the city, without any means of observing the rules of decency . . . they constitute one large forcing bed for the generation of vice,'[20] and Walsham described the gross overcrowding in these lodging houses. He said 'in the lodging houses 8 or 10 families, numbering from 20 to 40 individuals are sometimes to be found heaped together in the apartment.'[21]

The apathy of the governing body of the city that permitted unregulated building, and the continuance of the most primitive sanitary practices was not shared by all citizens. A voluntary body, the Carlisle Sanitary Association, was formed and sought, by exposing the evils of uncontrolled growth, to force Carlisle people to take a remedial action. The Associated stated the problem in a submission of evidence to Rawlinson:

the dwellings of the poor are too few in number and of faulty construction, being erected apparently with the view of having the greatest number in the smallest possible space, and without any regard to ventilation, drainage, and the necessary conveniences of life.[22]

The Association challenged all sections of the community. The owners of property 'have it in their power to remedy many of the evils loudly complained of by the poorer classes, but the labouring classes are not blameless.

> The Committee would be wanting in their duty to the artisan class if they failed to notice that many who are unfortunately obliged to live in dirty and otherwise objectionable tenements are by no means so limited in their resources as to be entirely helpless in the cause of sanitary reform.[23]

But the Association did more than exhort others to mend their ways. They took positive measures to remove the sanitary blots in the city. In 1831 voluntary committees were appointed, and the effectiveness of the system of biennial or triennial inspections, a system which originated in Carlisle but was copied elsewhere, was such that it was commanded by Dr Buchanan, in the ninth report that John Simon, one of the greatest Victorian medical officers, presented to the Privy Council in 1867.

> When Carlisle was perambulated by an officer of police as nuisance inspector we have three times as many cases of fever as when the town was systematically and simultaneously inspected in small sections by an equal number of organised committees.[24]

The voluntary Committee continued its activities until it was superseded by the regular city sanitary administration when a medical officer of Health was appointed in 1874.

Attention has so far been directed to the explosive population growth of early nineteenth century Carlisle and the congested low grade housing, with only the most primitive sanitary provision. But the more insidious, and potentially more calamitous problems connected with the unregulated growth of the city, were the related problems of the build up of sewage and refuse in the city streets, in the absence of a tolerable sewerage system, and the affects this had on the city's water supply. Reid outlines the city's sanitary state:

> Very few houses have proper necessaries, none are arranged to empty into drains; a few empty into cess pools, but the greater proportion are connected into ash pits. The contents are taken out in barrows [during the night] and carted away to farmers in the neighbourhood to whom they are sold . . . many of the inferior houses have no privies. There are no public necessaries.[25]

In addition to the problems arising from the accumulation of human detritus and that from pig sties, stables and cowsheds there was the objectionable feature of 18 slaughter houses in the city, chiefly situated in the courts and lanes without proper means of drainage. Dr Reid reported:

Clark's Court,
demolished to
make way for
Crown and Mitre
in 1905.
(*Tullie House*)

The accumulation of refuse is allowed to remain in open manure pits or heaps, the liquid part finding its way off by the surface channel or underground drains, or remaining in stagnant pools.[26]

To minimise the cost of cartage 'the manure pits were emptied when full!'

Another problem that was not adequately met at this time was a scavenging service for the streets and for dealing with household rubbish. Four scavengers were employed to clean the streets which were swept twice a week. But while the public streets were the responsibility of the Corporation, nearly the whole of the lanes and courts were private property, with which the Corporation had no effective power to interfere. 'Some were uncaved, and retained stagnant water, and the accumulation of the refuse thrown from the house.' The

Corporation had only power to intervene in private courts and lanes if a common nuisance was proved, which was often difficult owing to the inhabitants being unwilling to complain or give evidence against their neighbours, perhaps their own landlord.[27] In contrast to the nuisance of human and animal detritus, industrial waste does not seem to have been a problem in Carlisle. Dr Reid claimed 'there are none which materially effect the health of the inhabitants.'[28] The pollution arising from the increasing use of coal in factories and domestic promises is not mentioned in the reports. The nineteenth century town dweller no doubt became inured to smoke pollution, as did, a century later, the citizen of pre-World War 2 England.

Attention must now be directed to Carlisle's water supply, prior to the establishment of the Carlisle Waterworks Co. in 1847. Up to that time great use was made of a multitude of shallow wells, which as Rawlinson warned, were liable to be impregnated with the contents of cess pools, sewers and graveyards.[29]

Doctor Reid's report on Carlisle (2) refers to the 'total want of any extensive or systematic provision for the supply of water, beyond what is afforded from wells or the open river,'[30] and an additional limited supply was pumped, by means of a treadmill, from the river to the gaol tank, which was used occasionally for cleansing the streets or for extinguishing fires. Rain water was retained in casks and hard water was obtained by pumps. Doctor Reid noted 'In the higher and central parts of the city, the whole of the water is characterised by the very large quantity of earthy matter which it contains in combination with sulphuric and muriatic acids.' The water from the pumps in the lower parts of the town '. . . contains a much smaller quantity of earthy matter in solution, is consequently softer, and on that account is so far better adapted for general purposes . . . but, with scarcely an exception, even this is not sufficiently pure to render it either desirable or proper for the purposes contemplated.' Generally water for households use was sold from carts which, at 1d. for 8 gallons, made it a scarce commodity for a poor household.[31]

The absence of an adequate water supply had grave consequences for the sewage disposal methods for the city. There was under-drainage in a few of the main streets, but 'it is wholly defective . . . In consequence of the defective state of the sewers the corporation now refuse to grant leave for opening communications with water closets.'[32] One of the offensive features of Carlisle's sewerage system was the presence of open sewers around the city emptying into the rivers. The discharge of sewerage was most offensive. At the foot of Botchergate there was a mile long open sewer which discharged into the River Petteril. The fall of the gutter was badly graded with left stagnant pools. On the west of the city the 'Dam' extended from Slater's cotton mill through a most populous part of the town before emptying into the River Eden. 'It is a broad shallow stream of filth, proceeding from all the drains in the neighbourhood and it is a convenient place for the inhabitants to empty all sorts of washings into.' The Dam, which took surplus water from the mills, did not receive sufficient water to keep it clean. To the north west of the town 'a common sewer into which numerous water-closets etc. empty themselves forms an open gutter under the castle walk,' while another open gutter ran alongside the bridge embankment into the Eden. On the north-east of the town, at the bottom of Rickergate, there was another stagnant gutter which ran into the Eden. 'The blood from several killing shops ran into it.'[33]

When Dr Elliot spoke of the open drains encompassing the town[34] it was more than a mere fragment of speech, it was the literal truth. This is corroborated by the list of open drains and water courses which received the sewage of the city.

	Lineal yards
Botchergate drain	1,760
Caldewgate drain	660
Borough mill-dam	2,420
Little Caldewgate drain	4,400
Fisher St. drain	350
Rickergate, to river	220
	9,790

The width of the drains ranging from 1 to 1½ yards.

A dry factual account of the conditions under which thousands of Carlisle citizens lived in the nineteenth century are readily comprehended, and condemned, by the modern reader but it is more difficult to establish empathetic relationship with our forebears. The contaminated drinking water, the filth and the stench; the bedrooms and kitchens fouled by sewage, are fortunately outside our experience, and imagination cannot match the vividness of the original experience. Undoubtedly many Carlisle people were living under conditions that were a rejection of human dignity and a menace to the well-being of society but there is a gleam of hope visible in the 1840s. The first step to better things was the publication of the great social reports, in which slums were recognised as slums, and not as a norm of urban existence.

From the mid century steps were taken progressively to provide the city with a safe water supply and an efficient sewerage system, but first the effect of the sanitary horrors on the health of the citizens of Carlisle will be examined in some detail. These will be the topics of the next chapter.

NOTES

1. Friedrich Engels, *The Condition of the Working Class in England* (1842). Translated W. O. Hendersen and W. H. Chaloner, pp. 105–6.

2. D. V. Glass, *Development of Population Studies* (1975). Heysham's 'Observations on the Bills of Mortality in Carlisle for the year 1779 and 1787.'
3. R. Rawlinson, *Report to General Board of Health on City of Carlisle* (1850), p. 12.
4. Roper & Buggley's map of 1805 and Studholme map of 1842.
5. Rawlinson, op. cit., p. 91.
6. Dr Reid. Appendix Part II (Second Report). *Report on the State of Large Towns and Populous Districts* (1845).
7. Robert Rawlinson, *Report to General Board of Health on City of Carlisle*, (1850).
8. Sir John Walsham, *On the State of the Dwellings of the Labouring Classes* (First Report No. 24). Cumberland, Durham, Northumberland and Westmorland. Political Tracts. p. 1173 (1840).
9. Edwin Chadwick, *Report on an Enquiry into the Sanitary Conditions of the Labouring Population of Great Britain*, Political Tracts, p. 1172 (1842).
10. 'The Economist, a paper of exceptional intelligence, declined to go into details of the Public Health Act of 1848 and fill its column with a number of unpleasant works.' G. M. Young, *Portrait of an Age*, pp. 15–16.
11. Rawlinson, op. cit., pp. 54–5.
12. Rawlinson, op. cit., pp. 90–1 and pp. 101–3.
13. Ibid.
14. Rawlinson, op. cit., p. 51. A quote from the Report of the Carlisle Sanitary Association.
15. Ibid.
16. *Carlisle Journal*, 3 March 1819.
17. Reid, op. cit., p. 213.
18. Brown Street has now disappeared under the southern railway approach to the Citadel Station.
19. Reid, op. cit., pp. 214–15.
20. Rawlinson, op. cit., p. 56.
21. Walsham, p. 411.
22. Rawlinson, op. cit., p. 53.
23. Ibid.
24. Dr Henry Barnes. Presidential Address, Sixty-fourth annual meeting of the British Medical Association held in Carlisle 1896. *British Medical Journal July-December 1896*, p. 248. Dr Barnes was Physician to the Cumberland Infirmary, Carlisle.
25. Reid, op. cit., p. 216.
26. Reid, op. cit., pp. 215–16.
27. Reid, op. cit., p. 214.
28. Rawlinson, op. cit., p. 64.
29. Reid, op. cit., p. 207.
30. Reid, op. cit., pp. 215–16.
31. Ibid.
32. Walsham, op. cit., pp. 416–17.
33. Rawlinson, op. cit., p. 55.
34. Rawlinson, op. cit., p. 56.

CHAPTER 5

Disease and Mortality:
Water and Sewerage

to transfer the treatment of affairs from a polemical to a statistical basis, from Humbug to Humdrum.

G. M. Young[1]

It is a commonplace that mortality rates in manufacturing towns were unacceptably high during the Industrial Revolution and that, in particular, child mortality was horrendously high. The Carlisle historian is fortunate to have an unrivalled body of statistical date to make a quantitative analysis of mortality and disease in an early industrial society. It is possible to quantify mortality rates, to show how they varied over different age groups and to show in what classes, and in what localities, people were most at risk, and precise assessments can be made of what were the killer diseases of the late eighteenth and the nineteenth century.

Historians generally credit the great statistical inquiries into social conditions in Britain to the 1830s which were followed by the parliamentary reports of the 1840s, pre-eminent among which was Edwin Chadwick's Report on enquiry into the Sanitary Conditions of the Labouring Population of Great Britain (1842); but more than 60 years earlier Dr John Heysham,[2] a Carlisle medical practitioner began his demographic statistical observations to record, and analyze the annual births, marriages, diseases and deaths in Carlisle for the 10 years 1779 to 1788. The quality of Heysham's observations, and their relevance for actuarial purposes, was confirmed by their adaption by J. Milne, of the Sun Life Assurance office, as the basis of the Carlisle Life Table, a table so well founded that it was used by Assurance Societies down to the late nineteenth century.[3]

Heysham, a pioneer in the scientific investigation of disease and mortality in urban areas, chose to accept the route of painstaking, if humdrum, fact finding, in place of the specious generalisations of his time. His programme and purpose was:

The establishment of a judicious and accurate register of the births and burials in every town and parish would be attended with the most important advantages, medical, political, and moral. By such an institution the increase or decrease of certain diseases, the comparative healthiness of different situations, climate and seasons, the influence of particular trades and manufactures on longevity; with many other curious circumstances, not more interesting to Physicians, than beneficial to mankind, would be ascertained with tolerable precision.[4]

Heysham's figures for the years 1779–87, averaged by Milne are the basis of the Carlisle Life Table. The mortality rate, for different age groups, shows up in stark relief the horrendous mortality rate for young children. The rate for children from 0–5 years (8% p. a.) is 8 times that for children of 5–10 years (1% p. a.) and no less than 16 times that for children 10–15 years (0.5%). Another way of looking at this age differential is to observe that while the life expectancy of a child at birth is only 39, if the child survives the first year the life expectancy leaps to 46, with a further rise to 56 if the child survives to an age of 5. (See Table No. 1).

Milne's tables, averaged and grouped for actuarial purposes, are a very abstract presentation of Heysham's data. Thus while the mortality rate averaged over 9 years for the 0–5 year group is 8.22, the annual figure varies from approximately 5 in 1784, to 15 in the year 1779. The reason for this enormous variance, the unpredictable hazards of life in eighteen–nineteenth century England, are evident in the table No. 2.

There was a particularly virulent smallpox epidemic in 1779, and smaller ones in 1792, 1785 and 1787. In addition in the year 1779 there was a scarlet fever epidemic and measles epidemics in 1780 and 1786.

Dr Heysham, 1753–1834, who is said to have assisted Paley on the question of structural design in nature. (*County Library*)

Table No. 1: Mortality rates and life expectancy of different age groups in Carlisle, averaged over years 1779–1787

Age	Mortality rate p. a. %	Life Expectancy Remaining Years	Total Years
0)		38.72	39
1)		44.68	46
2)	8.23	47.55	50
3)		49.82	53
4)		50.76	55
5)		51.25	56
	1.02		
10		48.82	58
	0.50		
15		45.00	60
	0.69		
25		37.86	63
	0.90		
35		31.00	66
	1.26		
45		24.46	69
	1.48		
55		17.58	73
	2.95		
65		11.79	77
	5.44		
75		7.01	82
	12.53		
85		4.2	89
	24.58		
95		3.53	99

Table No. 2: Tables of mortality for Carlisle 1779–1787
Causes of death for children under 5 years of age

Year	1779	1780	1781	1782	1783	1784	1785	1786	1787	Total
Child population at risk	1,029								1,164	
Smallpox	86	3	17	28	17	9	39	1	28	228
Scarlet Fever	31									31
Measles		28	1					26	1	56
Thrush	2	12	9	10	6	6	11	11	8	75
Consumption	3	4	2	7	4	1	6	3	8	38
Weakness of Infancy	9	37	25	19	34	23	24	39	31	241
Subtotal	131	84	54	64	61	39	80	80	76	669
Total all deaths	150	103	68	78	73	46	96	109	89	812
Child mortality rate p. a. %	14.6	10.1	6.6	7.4	6.9	4.5	9.4	10.3	7.6	7.8

The 812 deaths for the 9 years for children under 5 is 44% of the total deaths (1840) for all age groups,, of the total population.

Smallpox was the only major epidemic disease of the eighteenth and nine-teenth centuries which was contained by medicine and in Carlisle advocacy of the practice of inoculation in its earlier form was, after initial hostility, particu-larly effective.[5] In his 'Observations' for 1779 Heysham reported that of the 300 people infected with smallpox during the last 6 months of the year no less than 90 died, whereas of the several hundred that had been inoculated in the neighbourhood of Carlisle not one of them had died. Yet he encountered great opposition to this practice.

> Yet so great is this prejudice against the salutary practice of inoculation amongst the vulgar, that few, very few, can be prevailed upon either by promises, rewards or entreaties to submit to this operation. No wonder that in rude, ignorant and barbarous times superstition hurried men into the grossest absurdities, when in a polished and enlightened age, in an age too, when the experience of full twenty years has already demonstrated the utility of inoculation, we see the bulk of mankind ready to sacrifice their children, and all that is dear to them, to a foolish prejudice.[6]

The attitude of the Carlisle people was more favourable in 1785, when the epidemic was again rife. The resolution of the committee of the Carlisle Dispensary that 'a general inoculation of the poor and indigent inhabitants will be attended with very beneficial effects' was made public by the common crier and 'great numbers from all quarters of the town flocked to the Dispensary to reap the benefits which it held out to them'. The outcome confirmed Heysham's judgement; every one of the 200 inoculated not only recovered, 'but had the disease in a very favourable manner'. Heysham calculated, on the basis that one in four who contract smallpox die, that 50 people had been saved by this general inoculation.

Yet too sanguine a view must not be taken of Heysham's early work in this field. Jenner's discovery of vaccination against small pox, published in his paper of 1798, was replacing the more dangerous method of inoculation in 1800. It is noteworthy that Heysham vaccinated his youngest daughter as early as October 1800 against the malady and henceforth 'continued the good work to all, without fee or reward'.[7]

Heysham viewed the health record of Carlisle with some complacency. He wrote in his 1779 report

> The air about Carlisle is pure and dry, the soil chiefly sand and clay. No marshes or stagnant waters corrupt the atmosphere; its neighbourhood to a branch of the sea, and its due distance from the mountains on all sides render its air temperate and moderate.[8]

In 1813 Heysham wrote to Milne in an optimistic vein

> I am of the opinion that the labouring classes of society have lived better

the last 15 years (the years of scarcity excepted) than from 1778 to 1788, and I also think that the mortality of late has rather diminished than increased in Carlisle . . . the people in general certainly now pay more attention to cleanliness and, upon the whole, live better than they did.[9]

But there were ominous portends. In 1781 Heysham records the appearance of 'a very epidemic fever, evidently the Typhus Carcerium' which raged almost exclusively in the city slums.

It however chiefly, I may almost say entirely raged among the common and lower ranks of people, and more especially amongst those who live in narrow, close confined lanes, and in small, crowded apartments . . . in the short space of almost eight months near 500 persons were effected with this fever, with 48 deaths.[10]

Heysham associated the disease with poverty, uncleanliness, and polluted air. He comments:

The outbreak occurred in a house in Richard-Gate which contains about half a dozen very poor families, the rooms are exceedingly small, and in order to diminish the window tax every window that even poverty could disperse with was shut up, hence stagnation of air which was rendered still more noxious by the filth and uncleanness of the people.[11]

Heysham, with the help of the Dean and Chapter of the Cathedral established the first dispensary for the poor of Carlisle in July 1782, and in the first 14 years the Dispensary treated 11,382 patients in the small room over the Abbey Gate. At a later date it was moved to St Cuthbert's Lane, where it was so recorded by Mannix and Whellan in 1847. The cases of typhus, or jail fever as it was then called, are published for each succeeding year in the 'Observations'. The figures suggest the containment of an epidemic of increasing severity.[12]

Year	Cases treated at Dispensary	Deaths in the City
1782	26	16
1783	37	5
1784	43	8
1785	95	9
1786	59	10
1787	252	14

Dr Heysham's innovative approach to the problems of public health are shown up in the accounts of the Carlisle Dispensary for the year 1.7.1787 to 1.7.1788.

The debit column showed the following items out of a total expenditure of £250.18.4.

	£	s	d
Spirits	4	3	0
Wines	20	2	4
Groceries	13	12	0
Disbursements to Apothecary	8	8	3
Drugs	69	8	0
Apothecary's salary	40	0	0
and	47	15	6

the last item being listed 'To subscriptions for the year ending on this day as yet unreceived, and doubtful whether they ever will.'[13]

Dr H Barnes wrote in 1896

Previous to that period few British physicians had the courage to order good food and good wine in cases of typhus. Instead of bleeding his patients Heysham found that by a copious and liberal use of tonics, cordials, stimulants, wine and bark, the pulse became stronger, the thirst and pain in the head abated, the delirium was removed and the patient got refreshing sleep. It was fifty years later before these views in regard to the treatment of fevers became generally accepted.[14]

The inauguration of the registration of births and deaths in 1837 permits a comparison to be made between the late eighteenth century Carlisle of Heysham's day with the much larger, and congested, industrial town of the mid nineteenth century. The comparison, decidedly unfavourable for Carlisle, with the mortality rate increasing and life expectancy decreasing, disproves the theory that the main factor in the rapid growth in the population of Carlisle in the first half of the nineteenth century was a decrease in the mortality rate.

Crude mortality rate p. a. %

	Heysham	Civil Registration	
	1780s	1838–44	1849–55
Carlisle	2.5	2.72	2.69
National average		2.19	2.17

The contribution of child mortality to the increasing overall rate is emphasised by a comparison of the life expectancy of a child at birth and at 5 years old using Heysham's figures and by making an estimate from Dr Reid's Carlisle Borough mortality table II.[15]

	Life Expectancy	
	At birth	For children over 5
Heysham 1779–1787	39	56
Reid 1843	27.1	48.5

It is to be regretted that neither Heysham or Reid provide an analysis of life expectancy for the different classes of society in Carlisle in such a stratified society, but Young's figures[16] for a wide range of industrial towns in the nineteenth century in Victorian England suggest that the social status, and the financial resources, of the parents are all important.

	Expectancy of Life at Birth			
	Derby	Leeds	Manchester	Liverpool
Gentlefolk	49	45	38	35
Traders and farmers	38	27	20	22
Labourers	21	19	17	15

Dr Reid's report provides valuable information of the prevalence of disease and the location of the 'fever dens' in Carlisle in the 1830s. He makes a statistical analysis of the 'Prevalence of thirteen Febrile Diseases in thirty-five districts of Carlisle', as recorded in the register of the Dispensary for four years in the period 1832–1841.[17] The statistics reveal a concentration of disease in limited, but well defined areas of the City. Four of the areas were in low-lying extra-mural areas. The 'low' areas were:-

1. Damside, i.e. the area contiguous to the old Corporation Dam. It included Irish and English Damsides, Backhouse Walk and extending southwards along the Dam to include Borough Street, John Street, Robert Street and S. George Street.[18]

2. Shaddongate.[19]

3. Caldewgate including Bridge Street, Church Street and John Street.

4. Willowholme.

The statistics given for the prevalence of Febrile Disease for the years between 1832 and 1841 were:[20]

Year	1832	1833	1838	1841
Botchergate and Lanes	304	311	126	134
Damside	118	129	159	151
Shaddongate	161	103	96	86
Caldewgate	179	167	100	117
Willowholme	92	68	61	30
Total of all 35 Districts	1,619	1,422	981	959

These five areas accounted for approximately 60% of the total cases for the thirty-five districts identified in the report. The Botchergate and Lanes figures were swollen in 1832 by the large number of cases of cholera in that district and in 1833 by a high incidence of influenza.

The two great cholera epidemics were confined almost entirely to the poorest, and correspondingly, the most congested and insanitary parts of the town. In 1832 there were 448 recorded cases of cholera with a mortality rate of one in three. In 1834 there was a second visitation with thirty-three cases, but a higher mortality rate of two in three.

Typhus was endemic in Carlisle in the low-flying districts. The periods 1837–38 and 1840–41–42 were particularly bad. The Report lists the locations from which fever patients had been taken to the Fever Hospital in the twelve years from 1831 to 1843. The same five areas named above were again among the black spots of the City accounting for 502 cases out of a total of 1223 (i.e. 41%).[21] In to this picture of unrelieved squalor and disease it is pleasant to report on one housing area for industrial workers, where the houses were clean and well cared for, the workers were well paid and epidemics absent. The area referred to is Trinity Buildings (Wigton Road) which contained a population of 362, principally employed by Messrs Dixon in Shaddongate. No cases of cholera or typhus were reported and the dwellings wee remarkably free of the other Febrile Diseases. Doctor Reid reports:

> The comparative healthiness of this place, where the dwellings are well constructed, and situated considerably above the level of the lower parts of the town, where cleanness is enforced, and where the operatives are comparatively well paid, as contrasted with that of any similar amount of the labouring population in the low parts of the town, or even of the lanes of the high level, is very striking.[22]

Typhus remained endemic in the city and additional facilities were required for the treatment of patients. A fever hospital, named the House of Recovery, was opened in Collier Lane in 1820 and this shared the burden with the Dispensary. In the 12 years 1832–1843 no fewer than 1143 cases of typhus fever were treated at the Fever hospital. The year 1838 was particularly bad with 265 cases, while the years 1840–1842 averaged 157 cases per annum.[23]

In this account of high endeavour by dedicated medical men in Carlisle to treat diseases, with causes as yet imperfectly understood, it must be recorded, with shame, that the Cumberland Infirmary in Carlisle was projected in 1828, but due to disputes it was not opened until 1841.

The basic facts of the occurrence of disease, the types, extent and the discrimination between localities, were established beyond any reasonable doubt by the mid nineteenth century, but the remedial steps to be taken involved not only a clash of interests but also a difference in emphasis on the fundamental causes of endemic and epidemic fevers. With hindsight it is not difficult to see the imminent dangers of the impact of industrialisation, and the explosive growth of population in a restricted urban setting with the gross overcrowding to which this led, and of the failure of the influential citizens to realise the deadly hazards of a polluted water supply when so little importance was attached to the removal of the detritus of man or animal in urban settings. Nor was there sufficient recognition, by national or local authorities, of the debilitating effect of the grinding poverty of large classes of people and the dangers that would ultimately present to all citizens, albeit to different degrees, whether they lived in a palace or a hovel.

Within the dichotomy between the burgeoning industrial society and the grinding poverty of the industrial worker, poverty had become synonymous with squalor. Heysham, referring to an outbreak of typhus in Carlisle in 1781 singled out poverty as a 'predisposing' cause, as distinct from the 'occasional' cause, which will be discussed later.

The occasional cause was evidently human effluvia, which as I had before observed was first generated in a house in Ricker-Gate. The predisposing cause were all of a sedative and debilitating nature, such as poor watery diet, uncleanness, cold, intemperance in drinking, excess in venery, fatigue, grief and anxiety, fear and previous diseases.[24]

No class was at greater risk than the hand loom wavers

The hand loom weavers are a numerous body, who have for many years worked for very low wages; their sedentary and constant occupation renders them liable to take disease more readily than those actively employed, but it is probable that this class are still more subject to disease from deficient food, and being crowded together in ill ventilated dwellings; they form a large proportion of the patients of the medical charities.[25]

By the middle of the century there was a strong body of medical opinion that named poverty as the greatest enemy of society. Dr Gregory wrote in the Lancet in 1843 'The greatest foe to health and long life is poverty,'[26] while Dr

John Hunter wrote in 1849 'If other causes have slain their thousands, poverty has slain its tens of thousands'.[27]

But problems of poverty were intractable in the foreseeable short and medium term future, while an effective attack on the unequal division of wealth was unrealistic in the prevailing political climate and in face of a restricted electorate, unrepresentative of the citizenship as a whole. It was to solutions to the 'occasional' causes of diseases, realisable in the short term, that attention must be directed.

The eighteen/nineteenth century attempts at a solution were misdirected but not rendered profit-less by a misconception of how the great fever diseases, typhus, typhoid and cholera were spread. The accepted view in the mid nineteenth century was the miasmic theory of disease transmission where the agent was 'bad air', ('Malaria') much in evidence in the effluvia from urban slums. Clear up the urban centre of offensive matter, thereby removing the bad smells, and all would be well. This view was held by the ablest workers in this field. Heysham in 1772 noted that disease was 'the offspring of filth, nastiness and confined air, in rooms crowded with many inhabitants'.[28] The same basic view was still held 70 years later. Chadwick in his report states:

> That the various forms of epidemic, endemic, and other disease caused, or aggravated, or propagated, amongst the labouring classes by atmospheric impurities produced by decomposing animal and vegetable substances, by damp and filth, close and overcrowded dwellings prevail amongst the population in every part of the kingdom . . .[29]

He contrasted the enormity of this avoidable expenditure in human life with the loss of life in wars

> the assumed loss of life from filth and bad ventilation is greater than the loss from death or wounds in any war in which the country has been engaged in modern times.[30]

The miasmic theory that disease was spread by 'sewer atmosphere' was accepted until the 1870s when it was replaced by the germ theory, advocated by Lister & Pastear, where the disease carriers were molecules of excrement and microscopical forms. The practical effect of the miasmic theory was beneficial by the stress it laid on cleanness, in that the removal of excrement and filth from the environment removed this breeding ground for flies and water-born germs. Professor Michael Flinn wrote:

> Miasma might not actually carry germs from a diseased to a healthy body, but in the absence of an exact and accurate knowledge of the means of infection, it was not a bad guide. The eradication of miasma – not entirely achieved even by the mid-twentieth century – was a sound instinct, and could do nothing but good.[31]

Edwin Chadwick in his report in 1842 showed the way in which industrial towns could escape from these conditions of filth and degradation, and at the same time he made out a strong economic case for doing so. He pointed out:

> As to the means by which the present sanitary conditions of the labouring classes might be improved . . .
>
> That the chief obstacles to the immediate removal of decomposing refuse of towns and habitations have been the expense and annoyance of the hand labour and cartage requisite for this purpose.
>
> That this expense may be reduced to one-twentieth or to one-thirtieth, or rendered inconsiderable, by the use of water and self-acting means of removal by improved and cheaper sewers and drains.[32]

Chadwick's proposed solution, the discharge of all refuse through a properly sewered system adequately supplied with water was admirable as far as it went, but the problem did not end there as Chadwick recognised:

> The chief objection to the extension of this system is the pollution of the water of the river into which the sewers are discharged. Admitting the expediency of avoiding the pollution, it is nevertheless proved to be an evil of almost inappreciable magnitude in comparison with the ill health occasioned by the constant retention of several hundred thousand accumulations of pollution in the most densely peopled district.[33]

The first positive step taken in Carlisle to obtain an adequate domestic supply of unpolluted water, which was also adequate to service a sewerage system of a type proposed by Chadwick, was the formation in 1846 of a joint stock company to supply the city with water from the River Eden at a point adjacent to its junction with the River Petteril.

A steam engine was erected at Stoney Holme, at the intake point, and the water after filtration was piped along Union Street and London Road to the highest ground in Carlisle at Gallow Hill, where a large reservoir was built with an estimated capacity of ten days supply. Mannix and Whellan report

> The principal buildings and manufactories in the town and neighbourhood can thus, at all times, have the command of a large body of water in cases of fire, which, as the mains will be constantly charged, can be obtained at a moment's notice, from the fire plugs being fixed at available distances; and posts can also be placed at convenient parts of the town to provide supplies for cleansing and watering the streets, and other purposes. It has been ascertained that there are in Carlisle 4481 dwelling houses varying in amount of rental from under £3 to upwards of £100 p. a.; and it is proposed that the poorest class of houses, viz. those under £3 rent, should have an

unrestricted supply of water at the rate of 1d. per week; the price for the higher classes gradually rising in reasonable proportion to the rental.[34]

A great improvement indeed from the 1d. for eight gallons of indifferent water which Doctor Reid had noted. The total cost of the schemes was estimated at £15,000 which it was proposed to raise in £10 shares. The initial response to the new water supply was equivocal. Mr Steel, the Chairman of the Water Company gave evidence to Rawlinson's committee

> The former mode of supplying the town was by pumps, and by carts carrying barrels. The carters charged one halfpenny per two tins-full, holding about 4 gallons, or 6d per cask of 100 gallons. At first we had some difficulty in inducing people to dispense with private pumps . . . there was, on the establishment of the works, coldness or indifference, rather than opposition to us.[35]

Soon advantage of piped water was seen. By 1849 760 private dwellings at £10 and above, and 2619 dwellings at under £10 were connected up to the supply,[36] a commendable 75% of the total number of houses.

The supply included connection for 49 water-closets and 20 baths in private houses.[37] A meagre response, but indeed up to the end of Victoria's reign w. c. s. were in the minority of the houses. One of the major Carlisle industrialists was however not slow to take advantage of the new supply. J. D. Carr expressed his appreciation of having to clean the boilers of his steam plant only once in 6–8 months, whereas before they had to be cleaned every 5 or 6 weeks.[38] A worrying reflection on what the citizen had become accustomed to drinking.

That the provision of a piped water supply was a necessary but not a sufficient means of cleaning up the urban environment in Carlisle was recognised by Rawlinson in his 1850 Report. He advocated that the Corporation should purchase the Waterworks for the benefit of the town. Only a civic authority would have the powers to manage and superintend sewers, water supply, gas,

Carlifle Difpenfary.

THE Small Pox, both natural and from Inoculation, being now pretty general in *Carlifle*, and likely to fpread ftill further, the Monthly Committee of the *Carlifle Difpenfary* are of opinion that a general Inoculation of the poor and indigent Inhabitants will be attended with very beneficial Effects.

PRESENT,

Rev. Mr. PALEY, Archdeacon of *Carlifle*, in the Chair.
Mr. FOSTER,
Mr. MITCHINSON,
Mr. ELWOOD,
Mr. MILBURNE,
Dr. HEYSHAM,
Mr. BLAIN.

RESOLVED.

1ft. THAT all fuch Perfons as come recommended by a Subfcriber fhall be inoculated Gratis at the *Difpenfary*.

2d. THAT the fum of 2s, 6d. be given to the Parents who are moft indigent, and who have three or more Children inoculated, as a Reward for nurfing them properly during Inoculation.

3d. THAT a Subfcriber of One Guinea fhall have the Privilege of recommending three Perfons to be inoculated, with the Reward; or five who do not require it; and fo in Proportion for any larger Sum.

4th. THAT the Privilege of being inoculated at the *Difpenfary* be continued till the 1ft of *January*, and no

Carlisle Dispensary notice. (County Library)

cleansing and regulation; and house drainage and house supply could then be carried out simultaneously with economy.[39]

The Corporation did not take over the water supply until 1865 but they commissioned Rawlinson to prepare and carry out a Water-carriage system of sewage disposal of the type that had been advocated by Chadwick some years earlier. The Carlisle scheme, c. 1856, which was one of the earliest carried out on this principle, necessitated the laying of a graded main sewer that emptied itself into the Eden below the city.[40] As the water intake was about a mile above the city an effective separation was anticipated between the drinking water supply and the sewage.

The next decade saw another major advance in Carlisle in the treatment of sewage by a land irrigation system, with chemical treatment. Dr Elliot, who a decade later in 1874 was to become the first Medical Officer of Health in Carlisle, a great sanitary reformer, is believed to have introduced the use of carbolic acid in the treatment of sewage. His innovation greatly impressed Joseph (later Lord) Lister who wrote in 'The Lancet' of 16 March 1867

> In the course of the year 1864 I was much struck with an account of the remarkable effects produced by carbolic acid upon the sewage of the town of Carlisle, the admixture of a very small proportion not only preventing all odour from the land irrigated with the refuse material, but, as it was stated, destroying the entoza which usually infect cattle fed upon such pastures.[41]

The crucial steps, i.e. the provision of a pure water supply and a modern sewage disposal system, in the eradication of water-born disease had now been taken much more remained to be done. This is evident from the mortality rates for the second half of the century.[42]

Period	Mortality rate p. a. %
1842–1848	Ranged from 2.43 to 4.39
1874	3.26
1875	2.92
1881	1.81

The year 1974 was exceptional but even the 1875 figure of 2.92 is much higher than this 2.49 figure of Heysham's day. The appointment of a Medical Officer of Health in 1874 appears to have been crucial. Dr Barnes in his presidential address of 1896 said:

> Many recent sanitary improvements have been carried out in Carlisle during the last few years, and it is a pleasure to state that the local authority which has charge of the sanitary administration of the city appears to be fully alive to its responsibilities. Several insanitary areas have been scheduled in the

course of town improvements; many noted 'fever dens' have disappeared
. . . all private ashpits have been abolished; an improved method of house
refuse disposal has been adopted, all private slaughterhouses have been closed,
and public slaughterhouses have been erected.[43]

As for the city's water

The supply is abundant, and has been improved upon from time to time as
a pure and wholesome water suitable for drinking and other domestic and
manufacturing purposes.

But at the end of the century continued vigilance to protect the water supply
was still necessary

As a river supply it is necessarily subject to contamination, there being a
considerable population on the drainage area above the intake, but there has
never been in Carlisle a case of cholera, enteric fever, or other zymotic
disease attributed to the drinking of Eden water.

The Water Committee were not however wholly satisfied and several schemes
were prepared, but not at this time accepted, for 'obtaining by gravitation an
adequate supply from a source beyond the reach of contamination'. But such
a scheme had to wait for the twentieth century.

The nineteenth century witnessed the fight for the health
of the city. On the one hand
great impersonal economic and
social forces caused a deterioration from the level of health
and amenity reached at the end
of the eighteenth century.
These forces were the massive
growth of population, the
overcrowding to which this
led, the absence of sewerage
provision by apathetic and
nescient civic authorities, and
the grinding poverty of large
sections of the population
whose livelihood had been undermined by the introduction
of machinery. Against these
forces were ranged the enthu-
siasm and determination of
dedicated men who pursued

Edwin Chadwick, 1800–1890. Sanitary reformer, Poorlaw Commission in 1836, Board
of Health 1848–54.

their individual campaigns until the public conscience was aroused by the Reports of the 1840s. During the century progress can be charted to a more healthy city by a series of intermittent, and piecemeal, initiatives highlighted by such events as the foundation of the Dispensary in 1782, the Fever Hospital in 1820, a piped water supply in 1846, a water carriage sewage disposal system in 1856. The appointment of a Medical Officer of Health for the city in 1874 was a recognition of the need for normative and enforced policy for the removal of objectionable sanitary hazards such as private ashpits and slaughterhouses. Concurrently there was, with the diversification of trade and the opening up of the city to the country, an appreciable reduction in the more extreme forms of poverty. The balance of the forces of decay and healthy growth however was such that it was not until 1881 that the recorded city's mortality rate dropped below the rate of the Heysham era at the beginning of the century.

NOTES

1. G. M. Young, *Portrait of an Age. Victorian England*, p. 28.
2. John Heysham MD (1753–1834) settled in practice in Carlisle in 1778 and resided there until his death in 1834. He was also a naturalist and his observations of the flora and fauna of his district were published in Hutchinson's History of Cumberland. He was intimate with the Cathedral dignitaries and is conjectured to have assisted Paley on the question of structural design in nature. Heysham is buried in the Cathedral; a memorial window to him has been placed at the east end of the south aisle.
3. Dr Williams Farr in the fifth report of the Registrar-General (1843) paid tribute to the work of Heysham and Milne:

    I avail myself of this opportunity to pay my humble tribute to the fairness of the Carlisle Tables; to Dr Heysham who collected these facts with so much care, and to Dr Milne, who cast these facts so judiciously to the purpose of life insurance.

4. J. Heysham, *Observations on the Bills of Mortality in Carlisle for the year 1779*. Printed in D. V. Glass, *Development of Population Statistics* (1973).
5. The early inoculation method, as used by Heysham, was to infect a healthy person with matter taken from a patient with a mild attack of smallpox. Disturbingly the transmitted disease did not always remain mild, and significant mortality did occur. A safer treatment was introduced by Jenner in 1798, who inoculated with infected matter from a patient suffering from the relatively mild disease of cowpox. This conferred immunity against the much more virulent smallpox.
6. Heysham, op. cit.; Observations, 1779, p. 6.
7. H. Lonsdale. 'Worthies of Cumberland' (1875), p. 260.
8. Heysham ,op. cit.; Observations, 1779, p. 1.
9. W. A. Armstrong, *The Trend of Mortality in Carlisle between the 1780s and the 1840s. A demographic Contribution to the Standard of Living Debate*, Economic History Review (1981), p. 104.

10. Heysham, op. cit.; Observations, 1781. p. 1.
11. Ibid.
12. Heysham, op. cit.; Observations, 1782–1787.
13. Heysham, op. cit.; Observations, 1787.
14. Henry Barnes' President's Address. Sixty-fourth Annual Meeting of the British Medical Association, held in Carlisle (1896). p. 250. Dr Barnes was physician to the Cumberland Infirmary.
15. Dr D. B. Reid, Carlisle, Report on its Sanatory Condition. Appendix from Part II of the Royal Commission's Report on the State of Large Town's and Populous Districts Second Report 1845. p. 208.
16. G. M. Young, Portrait of an Age. Victorian England, p. 21.
17. Reid, op. cit., Tables IV and V.
18. The Corporation Dam is clearly shown on the Roper & Brayley 1805 Map.
19. I have included Duke St., Broadguards and Queen St., in the triangle of land between Shaddongate and Caldewgate, in this area.
20. The Febrile diseases were listed as:

    Continued fever, Intermittent fever, catarrh and Influenza, Scarlet fever, Measles, Smallpox, Hooping-cough, Croup, Quinsy, Diarrhoea, Dysentery, Cholera, Erysipelas.

21. Reid, op. cit., pp. 207–16.
22. Ibid.
23. Ibid.
24. Heysham, op. cit.; Observations, 1781, p. 4.
25. Reid, op. cit., p. 213.
26. A. S. Wohl, Endangered Lives. Public Health in Victorian Britain. p. 46.
27. Ibid.
28. Wohl, op. cit., p. 145.
29. Edwin Chadwick, Report on an Enquiry into the Sanitary Conditions of the Labouring Population of Great Britain, House of Lords Political Tracts. p. 1172 (1842), p. 369.
30. Ibid.
31. Flinn (ed.), Report on the Sanitary State. p. 63, quoted from Wohl, op. cit., pp. 87–8.
32. Chadwick, op. cit., p. 370
33. Chadwick, op. cit., p. 48.
34. Mannix and Whellan, Directory of Cumberland (1847), p. 144.
35. Robert Rawlinson, Report to General Board of Health on City of Carlisle (1850), p. 64.
36. Rawlinson, op. cit., p. 74.
37. Ibid.
38. Rawlinson, op. cit., p. 73.
39. Rawlinson, op. cit., p. 78.
40. H. Barnes, op. cit., p. 249.
41. H. Barnes, op. cit., pp. 248–9.
42. H. Barnes, op. cit., p. 249.
43. Ibid.

CHAPTER 6

Law and Order

Let the civil government learn from hence to respect their subjects; let
them be admonished, that the physical strength resides in the governed;
that this strength only wants to be felt and roused to lay prostrate the
most ancient and confirmed dominion; that the civil authority is founded
in opinion; that the general opinion therefore ought always to be treated
with deference, and managed with delicacy and circumspection.

William Paley[1]

The early years of the nineteenth century were a period of industrial growth
with a rapid increase in material wealth and property; but the property
belonged to the privileged few, with the majority of the population poor and
some desperately so. It was a time of violence and disorder, with society
brutalised by the harshness of life and the squalor of urban slums. In an
increasingly polarised society the privileged sought to maintain their power and
sophisticated philosophical arguments were advanced to justify the status quo.
But in this same period the stability of society was being undermined by the
rapid growth of population, the immigration of heterogeneous racial elements
into the cities, and the increasing poverty and hopelessness of major sections
of the community which were to render the old principles of social control
unworkable. The pressure for change was to lead grudgingly, and step by step
in the first half of the nineteenth century, to a radical transformation of the
draconian theory, and practice of law enforcement and punishment to a more
pragmatic and humane system. The experience of Carlisle in the early decades
of the nineteenth century can be looked upon as an example, par excellence,
of the conflicts between the innate conservatism of the ruling classes and social
pressure from the poverty stricken masses which was to result in far-reaching
legislative action in nineteenth century England.

England at the beginning of the nineteenth century was a decentralised state,
with the central government having little direct contact with the mass of the
people. The responsibility for law enforcement rested on a three tier organisation: the magistrate, the constable, and the night watchman. The magistrate,
a man of substance, the owner of land worth at least £100 a year, was typically
a member of the gentry with the leisure to perform a public duty. He was,
by the nature of his unpaid largely independent of direct governmental control.
He was a Squire Allworthy[2] figure, a man of authority in his millieu, and a

Archdeacon Paley, 1745–1805. Famous for his teleological argument for the existence of God (the watch and the watchmaker analogy), and also for his austere utilitarian exposition of law enforcement and civic control. Portrait by George Romney, engraved by Sir William Beachey.

dispenser of patronage. The constable was normally an unwilling conscript, unpaid and untrained who served a term of duty of one year; but as richer members of the public could opt out of obligatory service by providing a substitute, the constable could be a hired man serving a protracted spell of office, with conceivably a gain in experience and competence. The watchman, an office of much greater antiquity than that of a policeman, dates back to the 1285 Statute of Winchester[3] when Edward I made appointments to ensure 'watching and keeping the peace in cities, boroughs and towns.'[4] But the watchmen in eighteenth and nineteenth century England did not command the prestige in keeping with his long lineage. He was often old and feeble, armed only with a staff and unwilling to face any determined trouble maker. Thomas Rowlandson's 'Past one o'clock' is a cruel caricature, and perhaps too generalised, but nevertheless provides an authentic glimpse of the early nineteenth century.

The machinery of law enforcement in this three tier organisation was inadequate to protect property in an age when, to the ruling class, property was sacrosanct. The Government resorted to the use of terror as a deterrent. Douglas Hay writes:

> The most recent account suggests that the number of capital statutes grew from about 20 to over 200 between the years 1688–1820. Almost all of these concerned offenses against property.[5]

Many of the offenses for which the capital sentence was pronounced were trivial in comparison with the enormity of the sentence, but for a nation that was not prepared to pay, or even to accept, a realistic police force, or to provide prisons for long term prisoners, the draconian sentences could be supported by the rational argument that if the deterrent value of the law could be looked upon as the product of the probability of being caught, and the severity of the sentence if caught, and if due to a totally inadequate police force the first factor was very low, the logic of the argument might well be that the punishment should be horrendously high. This concept of law enforcement and punishment now seems strange and remote but it would be pretentious to criticise it as the product of a barbaric society. A more informative approach would be to study the operation of late eighteenth century society's system of law and punishment together with the underlying intellectual assumptions of the age. The rationale of the Establishment of this time is no where better expressed than in the political works of William Paley, Archdeacon of Carlisle.

Paley, who wrote his influential works while carrying out his pastoral duties in the city, was a noted theologian, a writer on social problems, and a major figure in the eighteenth century intellectual world.[6] His views on law and order were notably similar to the Establishment of the day and his apologia for the policy of harsh deterrence is an unrivalled exposition of the philosophical basis of civil law, as applied to property. A study of his doctrines can explain, if not condone, the harshness of the law at this time. Another distinctive feature of his social/political philosophy, his advocacy of discretion in the treatment of the 'mob' is logically distinct from the treatment of the individual criminal and will be examined later in the chapter.

Paley's policy was quite explicitly directed to the prevention of crime and to the protection of property, not to the administration of justice to the individual, or to the demands of humanity. Paley wrote:

> The proper end of human punishment is, not to the satisfaction of justice, but the prevention of crime.[7]

From this premise, he could rationally assert

> Crimes are not by any Government, nor in all cases, ought to be punished in proportion to their guilt, but in proportion to the difficulty and necessity of preventing them.[8]

In the same vain he continued:

> Thus sheep stealing, house stealing, the stealing of cloth from tenters or bleaching grounds, by our laws sentence the offenders to sentence of death; not that these crimes are in their nature more heinous than many simple felonies which are punished by imprisonment or transportation, but because the property being more exposed, requires the terror or capital punishment to protect it.[9]

Paley, in the absolute priority he gave to deterring the law breaker opens a yawning gap between justice and crime prevention. He justifies this in his rigorous, but austere, logic

The security of civil life which is essential to the value and enjoyment of every blessing it contains and the interruption of which is followed by universal misery and confusion, is protected chiefly by the dread of punishment. The misfortunes of an individual, for such may the suffering, or even the death, of an innocent person may be called, when they are occasioned by no evil intention, cannot be placed in completion with this object.[10]

But after this extreme exposition of the principles of law and order Paley recognised that the rigorous application of these laws would 'become more sanguinary than public compassion would endure, or than is necessary to the general security.' He advocated that a degree of humanity, and of circumspection be introduced into the application of the 'law of England.'

By the number of statutes creating capital offenses, it sweeps into the net every crime which under any possible circumstances may merit the punishment of death; but when the execution of this sentence comes to be deliberated upon, a small proportion of each class are singled out, the general character, or the peculiar aggravation of whose crimes render them fit examples of public justice. By this expedient few actually suffer death, whilst the dread and danger of it hang over the crimes of many. The tenderness of the law cannot be taken advantage of. The life of the subject is spared, as far as the necessity of restraint and intimidation permits, yet no one will adventure upon the commission of any enormous crime, from a knowledge that the laws have not provided for its punishment. The wisdom and humanity of this design excuses the multiplicity of capital offenses, which the laws of England are accused of containing beyond those of other countries.[11]

The result of the application of this policy, Paley maintains, was that those who receive the sentence of death, scarce one in ten is executed.[12]

The theory of law enforcement has been given a rationalistic veneer by Paley, that exemplar of the eighteenth century 'Age of Reason'. But as Philips points out a system with 200 capital offenses coexisting with a very weak force for law enforcement, and with machinery for obtaining pardons to commute death sentences is basically irrational. In practice it was a system which depended on a costly private prosecution by the victim and a criminal procedure that made many acquittals possible on technicalities. 'This means that many offenses were uncaught; if caught unprosecuted; if prosecuted unconvicted; and if convicted, unhung because of the granting of a pardon.'[13]

The rigour of the law in defence of property, and the discretion employed by the magistrate to avoid the ultimate sanction is exemplified in two court cases reported in local newspapers in the year 1817. One report reveals that John Mattinson, a labourer, was apprehended in possession of a piece of white calico 'in a damp state as if taken from a bleaching ground.'[14] Mattinson was sentenced to seven years transportation although the full rigour of the law would have carried the death sentence.[15]

The other case was connected with the 1817 food riots, after warehouses at Sandsfield[16] and Monkhill were broken into, when it was suspected that grain was being exported to Liverpool at a time of food shortage. Two weavers, two women and a young girl, seen making their way into Carlisle with bags of meal, were arrested, and the constables also fired at another suspect who made his escape. After being tried and sentenced the two weavers were transported, the women sent to the House of Correction for 6 months, and the girl – the eldest of a fatherless family of ten – was imprisoned for a month.[17]

In the early decades of the nineteenth century the pressure of public opinion resulted in a drastic reduction in the number of capital offenses; whereas in 1820 there were over 200 offenses for which the death sentence could be imposed, during the 1820s and 1830s many capital sentences were withdrawn. By 1841 there were only eight crimes for which the death sentence could be prescribed and in practice executions were only carried out for murder.[18]

A major function of the forces of law and order, quite distinct from action against individual criminals, is the maintenance of social order, or to express it in emotive, but apt, terms, mob control. While the rigour of the law, tempered by the discretion of the magistrate might be defended on pragmatic grounds for the prevention of individual crimes, it was proved to be ludicrously ineffective for controlling crowd violence when the police force available consisted of 2 constables. Paley, writing in the secluded cloisters of Carlisle Cathedral. showed a remarkable prescience of the problems that were going to rise in the rapidly growing industrial society of the nineteenth century. He saw the danger of outward repression without gaining the consent, or at least the acquiescence of the people. In 1785 he wrote his famous dictum, quoted at the beginning of the chapter, that civil government must learn to respect the deeply felt 'rights' of their subjects, with the warning that physical strength resided in the people who are governed. Only the circumspect use of power would enable a country to be governed in conditions of civil peace, if not of political or economic equality, between its inhabitants. How this was to be achieved was a political problem. Paley posed the question

> . . . in what manner opinion thus pervades over strength, how a power, which naturally belongs to superior force is maintained in opposition to it, in other words, by what motives the many are induced to submit to the few, becomes an enquiry which lies at the root of almost every political struggle.[19]

He readily identified the danger of the poor combining against their oppressors. The danger would be intensified if large numbers of dissatisfied men settled in the same districts of the city, especially if they were engaged in the same trade. He wrote:

> the most frequent and desperate riots are those which break out amongst men of the same profession, as weavers – hence also the dangers of those great cities and crowded districts into which inhabitants of trading countries are commonly collected. The worst effect of popular tumult consists in this that they discover to the insurgents the secret of their own strength, teach them to depend on it against a future occasion.[20]

In Carlisle his presentiment was fulfilled in the 1820s when strong concentrations of destitute weavers had settled in Caldewgate and made it almost a 'no-go' area for the police. Paley's advocacy of circumspection had gone unheeded. The system of social control which had operated effectively in pre-industrial England was irrelevant in rapidly growing urban areas when the paternal figure of the magistrate could no longer be expected to influence, or even to know, the masses of the industrial poor. Crucial factors in a deteriorating situation were the explosive growth of Carlisle between 1790 and 1820 when the population doubled from 7,000 to 14,000; the great influx of Scottish and Irish immigrants with consequent loss of homogeneity in the Carlisle population; and a depression of wage rates amongst the weaving population. Over a few decades the magistrate/citizen relationship deteriorated from a situation where the magistrate was accepted as a paternal figure, who conceded the plebian concept of 'natural rights', that men had a right to the necessities of life at a price which they could afford to pay, in a mileau where the magistrate and townspeople acted as members of a close-knit community with a mutual respect for their individual roles, to a relationship where the interests of the ruling classes and townspeople were diametrically opposed, and where the magistrate and his two constables, no longer prepared to meet the mob face to face, had recourse to calling out the militia.

   This interpretation of a growing social conflict between irreconcilable interests is supported by the study of the food riots in Carlisle in the years 1795, 1812 and 1817 which J. Barnes has described in considerable detail,[21] and in the weavers' riots of 1820 and 1826. The Carlisle riots of 1795 occurred in a year of European famine and widespread food disturbances. In July rioting occurred in Carlisle after big rises in the price of grain and suspected exports of local grain by avaricious dealers through the port of Carlisle at Sandsfield. In spite of the seriousness of the riot there seems to have been a symbiotic relationship between the magistrates and the poor, with each side recognising a limit beyond which they should not transgress. Barnes writes

> In 1795, even though there may have been political agitators present taking advantage of the situation, the townspeople and the magistrates were still seen to be acting as members of a close knit community, the populace felt

that they had a right to adequate supplies of food at a fair price, and the magistrates and capital citizens were prepared to concede this by setting up subscriptions, supervising the distribution and attending to the repayment of monies collected by the enforced sales of grain.[22]

The 1812 food riots, coupled with unrest in the textile manufacturing industry, were of a more intractable nature. Warehouses at Sandsfield were raided, but unlike the disturbances of 17 years earlier the grain was not taken to Carlisle to be distributed at an equitable price; now the supplies were looted and unwanted supplies wantonly destroyed. Large crowds subsequently assembled at the Town Hall and in the resulting tension shots were fired by the military and a woman was killed.

By 1817 the attitude of the authorities to the poor was hardening. The 'right' of the poor to free or subsidised food was denied, it was now subject to the performance of public works, with a small wage paid from the proceeds of subscriptions. The attitude of the well to do was, as related in an earlier chapter, was expressed in the Parson and White History and Directory of 1829.

Charity would be more extensively useful if employed in providing work [i.e. public works] than if given in gratuitous largesses.[23]

The authorities, adopting a hard line, and no longer willing to make compromises, were suspected of employing spies and agent provocateurs to uncover the instigation of riots,[24] and magistrates resorted to the offer of £50 rewards for the apprehension and conviction of rioters rather than confront them face to face.[25] The long established system of law enforcement by magistrates, with a minimal public force, was clearly breaking down and was soon to be brutally exposed in the 1826 election riots. But the resistance to change was deeply rooted and in spite of considerable Governmental pressure, radical change was delayed until the late 1850s.

The ideological resistance to change, with the contention that a strong police force was inimical to liberty, is well documented. More mundane objections will be raised in due course, but first the philosophical case for liberty, and freedom from state interference, will be stated. Paley treated the case for the preservation of liberty as axiomatic, it was justified even if it could be shown that the provision of a military or civil force for law enforcement was more effective. He wrote:

The liberties of a free people, and still more the jealousy with which these liberties are watched, and by which they are maintained, permit not those precautions and restraints that inspection, scrutiny and control, which are exercised with success in arbitrary governments . . . least of all will they [the people] tolerate the appearance of an armed force, or of military law; to suffer the streets and public roads to be guarded and patrolled by soldiers;

or lastly, entrust the police with such discretionary power, as may make sure of the guilty, however they involve the innocent.[26]

The question of whether an adequate police force should be established became urgent in the rising tide of violence in populous districts in the early decades of the nineteenth century and was debated with considerable venom.

A revolutionary concept in the practice of policing, the replacement of the old thief catching type of policing by a new prevention force, was put into practice in London in 1825 with the establishment of a full time paid police force; but the concept was too radical for the Provincial cities and was not generally accepted and made effective until nearly three decades had elapsed. John Christian Curwen, a country gentleman and old 'Country Party' whip, and a long serving MP for Carlisle from 1790 had reflected the attitude of the local establishment, when he spoke in the House in 1809 to oppose a bill to provide a police force in Plymouth. Hansard reported

> Mr Curwen was always, upon constitutional grounds, jealous of the erection of boards of this nature, because they served to increase the patronage of the crown, which was already so enormous, and which was so systematically advancing, that in time scarcely any man could escape its grasp; because they involved an augmentation of the public burthen, which he hoped speedily to see retrenched, or the public would have reason to despond indeed; and also because they interfered with the authority of the independent magistracy of the County.[27]

While the extension of police powers and the provision of stipendiary magistrates were opposed on the grounds of liberty there were more down to earth reasons why the local gentry and magistrates opposed a new 'Science of policing.' They valued in the existing order the opportunity to wield power, to exercise their discretion, to maintain their position as a ruling class, and at the same time they wished to avoid the cost of a large police force. After all such a force was not necessary! Thus as Ferguson wrote concerning Carlisle

> Whenever it was proposed to augment the civil force of 2 constables, it was always successfully opposed by the Corporation on the grounds that there was a garrison at hand in the Castle which the magistrates would call in when the 2 constables were overpowered.[28]

But this laissez faire attitude by the civic authority was becoming increasingly under pressure by the 1820s in a rapidly growing industrial city with a polarised society of 'the haves' and 'have nots'. The festering grievances of the weavers came to a head with the notorious incidents in the hustings of the 1826 election. R. S. Ferguson traced the sequence of events in the columns of Hansard from the speeches of Sir Philip Musgrave and Sir Robert Peel,[29] an abridged version of which is given below. Sir Philip, the Yellow (Tory) candidate, had ventured into Caldewgate to canvass the voters. His answers to questions on his political views, and in particular about the Corn Laws, enraged the crowd and a riot ensued during which Sir Philip was forcibly put on a loom and given a lesson in the art of weaving, while his less fortunate friends and members of the Corporation present were ducked in the mill dam. The Mayor, accompanied by another magistrate, bravely went to the scene of the riot with the entire police force of the town, namely two constables, and read the Riot Act. The mob replied by capturing the Mayor and ducking the constables. A detachment of troops from the garrison of the Castle, who were called in, were stoned and some severely injured. Shots were then fired by the soldiers over the heads of the crowd, with the tragic consequences that a woman looking from her window was killed. The trouble boiled up again four days later and the unfortunate Mayor was assaulted and beaten so severely that for several days his life was in danger.

The City Corporation came under heavy pressure to take action to put an end to civil disturbances. Sir Robert Peel, Home Secretary in the Earl of Liverpool's Tory administration wrote to the Mayor of Carlisle, protesting about the situation, on 18 January 1827.[30] In the same year a committee of local Whig businessmen applied for a Police Act and were themselves elected as Police Commissioners with Home Office approval; which did lead to harmonious relations with the magistracy drawn from the Tory controlled Carlisle Corporation.[31]

Mr Batty, from Manchester, was appointed Superintendent of the new force with an establishment of 2 day officers and 16 night watchmen at an annual expenditure of £700. Every effort was made to distinguish the constables from the hated military, they were dressed in top hats, blue swallow-tailed coats and duck stove-piped trousers.[32]

The inauguration of the force was not auspicious. Mr Batty had served as deputy to Joseph Nadin of the Manchester police force and had been involved in the notorious Peterloo incident.[33] Batty's first venture into Caldewgate showed the helplessness of a civilian force of a Superintendent and two officers. Events were narrated by Parson and White

Mr Batty, and the officers under him, met with serious resistance from the Irish, Scotch and other weavers in Shaddongate when making their first survey of that part of the suburbs; when the then turbulent inhabitants, unused to the interference of an effective police, became so outrageous that it was necessary to call in the aid of the military and 150 Special constables by which means the riot was quelled, and 30 of the ring leaders taken into custody and punished. The officers have since exercised their functions without opposition, and peace and property are now as well preserved here as in any other place in her Majesty's domain.[34]

Military force had produced this salutary improvement but Parson and White's complacency was not shared by the Government and the military. On 26 October 1830 Major General Bouverie wrote to the Home Secretary complaining of the failure of the Corporation to keep the peace

> Both town and neighbourhood require to be under more effective supervision than is now the case, though how this is to be brought about is more than I am able to surmise.[35]

The tension between Government and Local Authority increased still further when, after effigy burning at the Town Hall, Lord Melbourne, Home Secretary in Grey's whig administration wrote to the Mayor of Carlisle on 8 December 1830 and expressed his utmost astonishment (at the events) notwithstanding the repeated representations that had been made, and criticised the Carlisle police as being 'so inefficient' and the magistrates 'so glaringly wanting in the performance of their duty.'[36]

The Government's representations were disregarded. The strength of the Force was not increased, and remained at 4 officers and 14 night watchmen even in the 1840s, although a new headquarters was built on the West Walls in 1840.[37] It was not until 1856 that new police forces, on the model of the Metropolitan Police, were established in all parts of England and Wales, and a new professionalism inaugurated by the appointment of Her Majesty's Inspector of Constabulary. It was only then in 1857 that the strength of the Carlisle Force was increased to 34 men.[38]

In the foregoing review of law and order in Carlisle no mention has yet been made of the Chartist movement that developed throughout the country in the late 1830s and which, Dr Barnes argues, took a strong hold in Carlisle.[39] This movement, for a few years, posed a great potential threat to the civil peace and stability of the country and alarmed government and local authorities.

The powerful stimulus given to the Chartist movement in the late 1830s arose out of the conjunction of the Reform Act of 1832, which in effect gave adult suffrage to the middle classes, and the New Poor Law of 1834, which by attempting to segregate the pauper from the 'more deserving' labouring poor, was greeted with fear and revulsion by all sections of the poor. Universal male suffrage was the primary principle of Chartism and thus it claimed political equality for the working classes; once this power had been attained radical changes could be effected in the economy and society.

The movement was inaugurated in Carlisle in July 1838 when Fergus O'Connor addressed a vast crowd, estimated between four and five thousands, who thronged around the Town Hall steps. The sequel was the setting up of the Carlisle Radical Working Men's Association, which from the beginning was almost exclusively of the 'lower classes' and in particular of hand loom weavers.[40] This meeting was the first of the many occasions that visits were made by Chartist leaders to Carlisle. The attitude of the leadership to the use of force was ambivalent. While initially much of the Chartist activity was peaceful and concerned with debating and petitioning, there were powerful voices who advocated the use of physical force, and as this faction gained the ascendency great concern was caused to the authorities especially during the great open air demonstration of 1839. The alarmed Carlisle magistrates reported to the Home Secretary in March 1839 that local Chartists were arming themselves with pikes and fowling pieces and were drilling at night.[41] At Whitsun 10,000 people took part in a meeting on the Sands but the arrest of the Chartists leaders and 'the presence in the town of two troops of the 2nd Dragon Guards had a sobering effect on the meeting'.[42] In August 1839 anxiety was again aroused in the town in anticipation of the forthcoming Chartist strike – the 'Sacred National holiday', decreed by the Convention of 12 August 1839. On instructions from the Home Secretary the Carlisle magistrates took the precaution of swearing in 900 Special Constables; 120 men of the Yeomen Cavalry were armed, and two troops of Dragoons were stationed in the Crescent; but in the event the strike passed off quietly.[43]

The peak of violence arising from the Chartist movement occurred in Newport in November 1839 when 3,000 Chartists were involved in an ill fated rising, and following military intervention 10 Chartists were killed.[44] The great national strike of 1842 found the Carlisle leaders divided, some encouraging the men to remain aloof but with others giving support. The magistrates responded to the threat by calling in the Yeomanry and Infantry, and by mobilising 200 Special Constables, but the strike was a failure and within a week all were back at work.[45] Thereafter there was a big fall off in support for the Chartist cause in Carlisle. The appeal was more to moral rather than physical force, and the seeking of middle class support was in itself a moderating influence. By 1848 'Temperance, Knowledge and Moral force' were the dominant themes in the local Chartist movement. Thus at the 1848 National Convention a Chartist delegate reported that his constituents in Carlisle were now of the opinion 'that nothing could be gained by physical force'.[46] The threat of insurrection was no more than a memory after 1850.

The corollary of a more efficient police force, and the abandonment of the expeditious despatch of felons by capital punishment or transportation was the formation of a comprehensive detention system to deal with criminals. Starting from a very low base improvements were effected in the prison service in the first half of the nineteenth century. The first step was the factual assessment of prison conditions at the end of the eighteenth century which stirred the public conscience. The information about the Carlisle prisons was both comprehensive and vivid.

At the turn of the century the County Gaol at Carlisle was

old, much out of repair, and without the regular means of supplying the different rooms with fresh air, so necessary in these wretched receptacles of guilt and misfortune.[47]

John Howard the celebrated philanthropist visited the County Gaol at Carlisle. His description might well have been taken from the 'Beggar's Opera'.[48]

He deplored the squalidness and the absence of segregation for men and women.

> The wards for felons are two rooms, down a step or two; dark and dirty. One of them, the day room, had a window to the street; through which spirituous liquors, and tools for mischief, might be easily conveyed, but it is now bricked up; the night room is only 11 feet by 9. At my last visit men and women were lodged together in it. Two rooms over the felons wards, which have been used as tap rooms, seem to be intended for women only, but in one of these I also found three men and four women lodged together.[49]

Howard found the furnishings, and the hygiene of the prison primitive. He described what he had seen

> The furniture is provided by the prisoners, and is generally wretched in the extreme. Mr Mallinder, the present gaoler, seems, however, to keep the different apartments as clean and comfortable as circumstances will admit. The rooms and passages are whitewashed once a year; the felons' rooms (wholly composed of stone) cleaned of all noxious matter, by burning a large quantity of straw upon the floor, so that disorders rarely prevail there. We would, however, recommend a more frequent use of lime as a wash: being convinced that, nothing is more conducive to the prevention, or eradication of infections.[50]

The dichotomy in society, between the 'haves' and 'have nots' was in evidence in the County Gaol. The possession of money enabled the prisoner to rent a room, to purchase milk and vegetables in abundant quantities, and seemingly at one time to obtain ale and spirits.

The County Gaol to which felons were sent was under the control of the Secretary of State for the Home Department. But in addition there was in Carlisle, until the city gates and wall were demolished, a local prison, housed over the Scotch gate, under the responsibility of the local justices in Quarter Session, where city debtors were confined. The debtors, during their incarceration, were given, or perhaps took, considerable licence. They were allowed the use of the turret of the gate house, and from this advantageous position demanded toll from the countrymen bringing peat to the market on pain of being bombarded with 'sundry stones which, from the decomposed effect of time were ever ready at hand for such a purpose.'[51]

The first major step forward was the passing of 'The Gaols Act' of 1823[52] which compelled the justice to classify prisoners so that steps could be taken to prevent the corruption of the good by the bad prisoner. This change in attitude, signifying a concern for the reform, as well as the appropriate punishment of prisoners, was expressed in a clause in the Act

> Prisons to provide for safe custody . . . and preserve health and improve morals of prisoners, and ensure a proper measure of punishment to convicted prisoners.

A radical transformation of the prison service in Carlisle followed within a few years of this Act. Jefferson reported on a striking new building which superseded the old gaol. 'The new Country Gaol and House of Correction was completed in 1829. A much bigger building with a lodge and offices which occupied the side of the old gaol.'[53] Mannix and Whellan gave more detail

> The new building consists of a centre and two wings, finished with an embattled parapet, and has several narrow Gothic windows to correspond with the court house to which it is united. Its front measures 340ft., and the entrance is through a beautiful pointed arch, with massive iron-studded doors, and over the gateway is an excellent clock for the convenience of the inhabitants. The interior buildings consist of the governor's house, and six radiating prison wings, affording accommodation for thirteen classes of prisoners, with separate airing grounds, so planned and divided by walls and lofty wrought iron rails, that the governor, and his assistants have, from their apartments, a complete view of the whole; and the improved system of prison discipline and classification is adopted. The prison contains room for 150 prisoners but there are seldom more than eighty at a time.[54]

The new prison in Carlisle anticipated the Prison Act of 1839.[55] The provisions of this Act called for new concepts in architectural, and social, engineering. One very important concept, concerning the avoidance of contamination of prisoners convicted of minor offenses with hardened and incorrigible prisoners was the classification of prisoners. The Act called for the division of prisoners, of each sex, into at least 6 classes, who were to be regulated and controlled by their own set of regulations. The new Carlisle prison appears to have been well equipped to meet the requirements of the new Act. The striking design of the prison is evident from its ground plan on the 1842 map of Carlisle. This review has recorded important changes in the domain of 'law and order' in the early nineteenth century. After long dissension the advantage of a system of maintaining order through a disciplined police force under civil power, rather than having to call upon the militia when civil disorder had got out of hand, had prevailed, and arguments about the alleged loss of liberty and local autonomy, and the 'intolerable' burden on local pockets had been finally discounted. In the practice of law enforcement the concept of prevention was given priority over the concept of punishment and the 'new' police force, schooled in the doctrine of law keeping and crime prevention replaced the old 'thief takers'. The horrendous sentences designed to act as a deterrent, as envisaged by Paley, were replaced by custodial sentences, the duration of which were matched to the seriousness of the crime. In the theory of imprisonment the idea of a revengeful society making the miscreant pay for his misdeeds was replaced by a policy with the emphasis on changing the behaviour of the individual offender by reforming him, by making him penitent with the ideal of isolating him in a cell of a penitentiary away from the corrupting influence of the hardened criminal. The substitution of penal servitude for transportation proved a key decision in the reform of the criminal code.

It can be convincingly argued however that crime and disorder in the period under review were primarily determined by the sheer poverty of large sections of the population in an uncaring society, and as poverty did not suddenly disappear the root cause of crime remained; but this in no way discounts the contention that society by the mid nineteenth century was a more humane society, and more efficient in social organisation than at the turn of the century.

NOTES

1. William Paley, *Principles of Moral and Political Philosophy* (1785), p. 410.
2. Henry Fielding, *Tom Jones*.
3. 13 Edward I.
4. The Act commanded that in 'every city six men shall keep at every gate; in every Borough twelve men; in every town six or more according to the number of inhabitants; and shall Watch the Town continually all night from the sub-setting unto the sun-rising.

   The use of the term 'watch' has been extended into modern times – thus the Watch Committee is responsible for the police force.
5. Douglas Hay, *Albion's Fatal Tree – Crime in Society in Eighteenth-Century England* (1975) p. 18.
6. William Paley was perhaps best known for his books 'View of the Evidences of Christianity' (1974) and 'Natural Theology or Evidence of the existence and attributes of the Diety collected from the Appearance of Nature' (1802) in which he used his analogy of the watch and watchmaker in the teleological argument for the existence of God. But Paley was also a political philosopher and his 'Principles of Moral and Political Philosophy' (1785) was both an advocacy and apologia for the policy of law and order in eighteenth-century England.

   Paley is buried in Carlisle Cathedral and his memorial stone can be seen in the north aisle of the choir.
7. William Paley, *Principles of Moral and Political Philosophy* (1785), p. 526.
8. Paley, op. cit,. p. 527.
9. Paley, op. cit., p. 529.
10. Paley, op. cit., pp. 552–3.
11. Paley, op. cit., pp. 533–4.

12. Paley, op. cit., p. 532.

13. David Philips, *Law Enforcement in England, 1750–1830*, from *Crime and the Law – Social History and Crime in Western Europe since 1500*, edited by V. A. C. Gatrell, B. Lenman and G. Parker, p. 158.

14. *Carlisle Journal*, 18 January 1817.

15. The harshness of the law at this time is implied by two legislative measures taken some years later to ameliorate the severity of the law. An Act of 1823 (4 Geo. IV c. 45) empowered courts to abstain from pronouncing the sentence of death on persons convicted of any felony except murder. An Act of 1832 (2 & 3 Will IV c62) repealed the capital sentence for larceny; whereas before it had been pronounced for stealing property worth more than £5; and the lesser sentence of 'transportation beyond the seas' was substituted for the death penalty for the stealing of horses, cattle and sheep.

16. Sandsfield, on the River Eden estuary, was the port for Carlisle at this time.

17. June Barnes, *Popular Protest and Radical Politics Carlisle 1790–1850* (unpublished Ph.D. Thesis, Lancaster University, 1981), p. 96.

18. Philips, op. cit., p. 156.

19. Paley, op. cit., pp. 406–7.

20. Paley, op. cit., pp. 412–3.

21. J. Barnes, op. cit., Chapter 3.

22. J. Barnes, op. cit., p. 107.

23. *Parson and White Directory* – quotation in Carlisle Museum file.

24. J. Barnes, op. cit., p. 100.

25. J. Barnes, op. cit., p. 97.

26. Paley, op. cit., pp. 541–2.

27. Parl. Deb. (1809), XII col. 1148, quoted by Philips, op. cit., p. 175.

28. R. S. Ferguson, *Cumberland and Westmorland MPs 1660–1867* (1871), p. 250.

29. Ferguson, op. cit., pp. 248–50.

30. J. Barnes, op. cit., p. 102 and p. 122.

31. Ibid.

32. W. H. Lakeman, *Watch Committee* from *Local Government of City and County Borough of Carlisle 1158–1958* (1958), p. 51.

33. J. Barnes, op. cit., p. 102.

34. Parson and White, op. cit., p. 130.

35. J. Barnes, op. cit., p. 102.

36. J. Barnes, op. cit., p. 106 quotes a letter from Lord Melbourne to the Mayor of Carlisle 8 December 1830 C.R.O., D/Ca/Civil disturbance file.

37. Mannix and Whellan, *Directory of Cumberland* (1847), pp. 119–20.

38. Lakeman, op. cit., p. 52.

39. At the height of the Chartist agitation there was a membership of between 2,500 and 3,000 in Carlisle at a time when the total population of the city was only 20,000. J. Barnes, op. cit., p. 328.

40. J. Barnes, op. cit., p. 325.

41. J. Barnes, op. cit., p. 339.

42. J. Barnes, op. cit., p. 340.

43. J. Barnes, op. cit., pp. 342–3.

44. J. Barnes, op. cit., p. 345.

45. J. Barnes, op. cit., pp. 356–8.

46. J. Barnes, op. cit., p. 364.

47. W. Hutchinson, *History of the County of Cumberland* vol. II (1794), p. 680.

48. John Gay's, *Beggar's Opera* (1729).

49. Hutchinson, op. cit., pp. 680–1.

50. Ibid.

51. M. E. Nutter, *Carlisle in Older Times* (1835), p. 26.

52. 4 Geo. IV c 64.

53. S. Jefferson ,*History and Antiquities of Carlisle* (1838), pp. 287–8.

54. Mannix and Whellan, op. cit., p. 124.

55. 2 & 3 Vic. c 56 (1839).

CHAPTER 7

The Coming of the Railways

We who lived before railways and survive out of the ancient world
are like Father Noah and his family out of the Ark.

Thackeray[1]

A great transformation in the lives of English people was inaugurated in the
early years of the 1830s. If this radical change could be symbolised by a
single event, that event must surely be the opening of the Liverpool-Manchester
railway in 1830. This year becomes the great symbolic dividing line between
an age when the speed of inland communication, and the volume of trade,
either by road or canal, was tied to the speed and strength of a horse, and an
age when steam power became the great new force which would revolutionise
transport. For Thackeray those who could remember the pre-railway age now
lived on severed from the world of their youth like Noah and his family after
the deluge.

The coming of the railway to Carlisle was to make a major impact on the
lives of the Carlisle citizen and industrialist. For the Carlisle industrialist inland
transport had been on a predominantly east-west axis. In the textile trade raw
cotton was imported via Liverpool, and the finished products were sent to the
great cotton markets of Manchester, via the sea route to the Solway Firth from
where they were transported and conveyed by road, or canal, eastward to
Carlisle. The imports of grain, timber and fuel and the considerable trade with
Ireland and Newcastle relied on east-west inland communication. In the 1840s
there was a radical re-orientation of communication lines to a north-south axis
resulting from the opening of rail links to London and Glasgow. But the
railway companies, with their wider horizons, but also bitter rivalries, and now
entering into the 'big league', were no longer responsive to the wishes of the
Carlisle industrialists, who were forced to enter upon hazardous, and almost
disastrous, ventures, to protect their trade routes. On the positive side the new
rail links permitted a new and diversified industry to grow up and to free
Carlisle from its dangerous over dependence upon the fortunes of the cotton
industry. For the ordinary citizen, within a decade of the inauguration of the
rail link to Newcastle, the whole country was opened up. He could now reach
London in 11 hours, Glasgow and Edinburgh in 3 hours. Soon he was to have
his own seaside resort at Silloth for the cheap day trip, or for a more extended
stay at one of the many holiday lodging houses or hotels. The middle aged

citizen living in Carlisle in the 1860s was conscious of living in a very different world to that of his youth. It is this momentous transformation, and broadening, of the life of Carlisle, with the impact on industry and society, occasioned by the introduction of steam power, that will be examined in this chapter.

By the late 1820s the Carlisle canal was well established, but had not met Carlisle's, or Newcastle's ambition for a link between the North and Irish Seas. In 1824 a committee formed in Newcastle to promote either a canal or railway commissioned Chapman to inspect the route and vie alternative estimates. His figure, of £888,000 for a canal and £252,000 for a railway, confirmed that the canal was no longer a viable alternative.[2]

An Act for making and maintaining a railway, or tramroad, from the Town of Newcastle-upon-Tyne in the County of the Town of Newcastle-upon-Tyne to the City of Carlisle in the County of Cumberland, with branch thereout . . .

was submitted and passed in 1829.[3] The purpose as set out in the preamble was

To facilitate the conveyance of lead, coal, lime, slates and other products of the land, and articles of merchandise from remote parts of the counties to the Port of Newcastle and City of Carlisle – and to facilitate the conveyance of manufactured goods and foreign merchandise between Newcastle-upon-Tyne and Carlisle.

The railway was to run to the north west corner of the canal basin in Carlisle. But what was envisaged was literally a railway without the later connotations attached to that word. The Act was quite specific 'No locomotive or movable steam engine shall be used – for drawing wagons on other carriages.'

Further restrictions were applied on the landed estates. 'No steam engine shall be erected or used within view of the Castle of Naworth or Corby Castle . . .'[4]

The present Newcastle to Carlisle line with its sharp curvatures still bears traces of a pre-steam locomotive age. The Act authorised the raising of £300,000 for the scheme made up of £100 shares, and provision made for the borrowing of an additional sum of £100,000 by mortgage if necessary. The rates for the Company, specified in the Act, were especially favourable for the landed interests. For example, manure, lime or road repairing material were 1d per ton per mile, but coal, ores, stones, timber 1½d per ton per mile and coke, bricks, flags, metals etc., 2d per ton per mile. These rates were similar, but for coal and timber somewhat less than those permitted by the Canal Act of 1823. The railway was built in sections, the Carlisle to Blenkinsop Colliery Greenhead section was completed in 1836 and the complete line opened in 1839. But the significance of the Manchester and Liverpool railway of 1830 had not been missed, the Act was modified and the line opened up to steam locomotives.

The line had a dramatic effect on the price of coal in Carlisle which dropped from 17s. a ton to 10s. a ton.[5]

The Carlisle Canal Company, who had welcomed and encouraged the railway to terminate at the canal basin, had judged correctly the initial effect of the railway, with a 100% increase in tolls between 1836 and 1840 and a dividend increase from 1% to 4%. The new link not only permitted the movement of goods from the north east coast, but also from the continent to north west England and Ireland, and the route was used by German emigrants on their way to Liverpool and to America in the great emigration wave currently taking place.[6] The fortunes of the Canal Company, boosted by the complementary activities of the Newcastle and Carlisle Railway Company, reached their apogee in the late thirties. Jefferson in his History published in 1838 wrote:

> The number of vessels belonging to the Port [Port Carlisle] is forty-four. The vessels employed in the coasting trade in 1836 were 831, the tonnage amounting to 68,855; in 1837 the number of vessels was 1186 and the tonnage 84,910. The increase is to be attributed to the railway communication with the Earl of Carlisle's and the Blenkinsop coal-mines.[7]

The day to day scene at Port Carlisle at this time was one of considerable animation. The exports were chiefly lime, free stone, lead and agricultural products, and the original conception of the import of coal from the Port had been reversed with the export of coal from East Cumberland to the Port and thence to Scotland and Ireland.

The Carlisle canal, for the first two decades of its existence, proved to be highly beneficial to Carlisle's industrialists and traders. Mannix and Whellan claimed that it

> . . . contributes greatly to the wealth and prosperity of the city by affording a communication with the Eastern ocean . . . It has a good trade in timber,

Wetheral Railway Bridge, built before power machinery was available.
(*Tullie House*)

iron, slates, etc., etc., and the exportations consist principally of grain, flour, meal, oak bark, alabaster, freestone, lead, staves, etc. The cotton wool manufactured here is brought directly from Liverpool, whither a great part of it is returned in a manufactured state for exportation.[8]

The connection to the Solway, to open up trading routes, had dominated the thoughts of the Carlisle industrialist during the first two decades of the Canal's existence. A subsidiary, but still vital, component of this conception was the rail link to Newcastle to link up, in the terminology of the day, the Western and Germanic oceans. The full significance, and capability, of the railway, with the steam locomotives as its power source, was slow to gain recognition, the vulnerability of the Carlisle canal as a trading artery was becoming only too apparent by the mid 1840s.

The Maryport and Carlisle Railway Co., authorised in 1837[9] and commissioned in 1845, with a superior port at Maryport, offered a challenge to the Canal Co., but one they could live with, but it was a new threat of north–south rail routes, combined with the machinations of railway politics, that was to constitute the great threat to the Company.

The Carlisle industrialists had invested considerable sums in the Canal, and were shortly to strain their resources in the conversion of the Canal to a railway and in a complementary venture to open up an entirely new port at Silloth. On other railway projects they had invested money in the Carlisle-Newcastle Railway but not to such an extent to exert influence on its future policy. Their financial interest in the Carlisle-Maryport Railway was minimal and control was in the hands of the West Cumbrians. Now when the next great challenge came in the opportunity to invest in the proposed Carlisle-Lancaster railway, as part of the link between London and Scotland, the chance to participate in the scheme was met with local apathy. After a year's delay the Cumbrian landed families, and the Dixon family, finally invested, but not sufficiently to obtain control of the Company's policy. On the great new north-south routes now to be constructed the policy of the North-Eastern Company was damaging in effect, if not in intent, to Carlisle's interest, while the western railways, eventually to be merged into the London and North Western, had a shadowy policy that did not protect Carlisle's industries.

The Western railway was however to assume so great an importance in the later development of Carlisle, industrially, commercially and on an individual level, that its genesis in North West England as the Lancaster and Carlisle railway deserves close examination. On the engineering and organisational level the construction of the railway was a prime example of mature Victorian achievement, but on a labour relations level it was but one more chapter of nineteenth century social division and exploitation.

Unlike the Carlisle-Newcastle, and Carlisle and Maryport railways the proposals for a north-south route through Carlisle had a national rather than a local significance and from the mid 1830s to the mid 1840s the debate was whether the line to connect London with Edinburgh and Glasgow should follow an east or a west coast route. The protagonists of the east coast route made the early running, but a lone voice, in the editorial of the *Carlisle Journal* of 1835, commenting on a proposal for extending the line from London to York into Scotland, argued strongly that the west coast route through Carlisle gave the greatest national advantage. Undoubtedly a line from London, via Birmingham and Preston to Carlisle and on to Glasgow would connect up the great industrial areas of the Midlands, Lancashire and the Scottish lowlands. The east coast route through Yorkshire, Durham coalfield and Tyneside could not command a comparable industrial catchment area.

The position in 1840 was that the London-Birmingham railway, continued by the Grand Junction line, connected with the Liverpool-Manchester line at Newton and from there connected to Preston by the North Union line.[10] In the summer of 1840 the west coast route was extended by the Preston-Lancaster line to Lancaster and by this time there was a continuous line from London to York on the east coast route. The government of the day, while considering the choice of routes to be of sufficient national importance to necessitate governmental intervention, had not yet appreciated the magnitude of the potential traffic between England and Scotland and judged that one route only could be justified. The option was which route to support. The 4th Report of the Royal Commission appointed to examine the proposals, issued on 13 March 1841 came out, conditionally, in favour of the west coast route.

> Seeing the extent of capital that would be required for the construction of 2 distinct trunk lines, one to Edinburgh and the other to Glasgow, we feel under the necessity of recommending at present the construction of one line only . . . We give the preference of one line from Carlisle to Lockerby, Lanark, Hamilton to Glasgow.[11]

But the recommendation was on the assumption that the line Lancaster to Carlisle was built; if it was not, and a party was found to construct the line from Darlington to Edinburgh, the western line should be abandoned for the present and the east coast line should have preference.[12]

The response in Cumberland and Westmorland to this challenge was apathetic. The *Carlisle Journal* reported:

> It required much time, much argument, and much canvassing to induce persons to take up shares; and it was not until the London and Birmingham and the Grand Junction Railways had undertaken to take shares to this amount of £350,000, on condition that other sums should be raised in the counties of Lancaster, Westmorland and Cumberland, that the scheme could be said to be fairly afloat. The North Union and the Lancaster and Preston Railway Companies also subscribed £60,000 each.[13]

Conran Cut, 1838. The first class carriage is roofed. There was no protection from the whether for the third class passengers or rail crew. (*Tullie House*)

In the course of 1842 a Parliamentary Survey of the whole line between Lancaster and Glasgow was vigorously prosecuted under the direction of Messrs Locke and Errington. Three schemes, each with their champions, were put forward and examined.[14]

Scheme 1 – the coastal route from Lancaster, across Morecambe Bay and the Duddon sands by means of an embankment, thence up the west coast of Cumberland to pick up Whitehaven and Workington and to connect up with the Carlisle-Maryport railway then under construction. This scheme was favoured by George Stephenson who justified the extra expense of the route by the value of the land reclaimed from the sea. The great engineering difficulties of that route however made it unattractive to all except the residents of West Cumberland.

Scheme 2 – was a line from Lancaster to Kendal and thence by the valley of Longsleddale and by Hawes Water to Penrith and thence to Carlisle. This presented formidable engineering problems in tunnelling below the Gatescarth Pass, and environmentalists must be thankful that this route was not chosen.

Scheme 3 – was for a line from Lancaster to Kirkby Lonsdale and thence by the valley of the Lune to Penrith, and from there to Carlisle. This scheme

THE DANDY—PORT CARLISLE

Port Carlisle 'Dandy'. Steam locomotives withdrawn from Drumburgh Junction to Port Carlisle line in 1857, replaced by horse-drawn carriage until 1914. First class passengers inside, third class on longitudinal forms outside and luggage on roof (similar segregation to stage coach).

was finally selected but amended so that the line would embrace Kendal with a cross over from the valley of the River Kent to that of the River Lune at Grayrigg. Preparations made to apply to Parliament fro the necessary Acts were frustrated in 1843 due to certain technical difficulties, but more importantly due to the apathy of those in Cumberland and Westmorland who had been expected to become shareholders in the Company, and the bill was delayed for a year.[15] But the great efforts now made to arouse public participation met with success so that at the end of the year the quota for Cumberland and Westmorland was guaranteed; the railway companies subscripted £500,000, and it was proposed to borrow £200,000 to make up the £800,000 which was now deemed sufficient to build a single line when it was found possible to avoid a tunnel through Shap Fells. A prospectus was issued in which a return was calculated of 7% upon the capital, the London subscription list filled up rapidly, and in a short time the whole of the shares were taken up, the amount thus raised enabled the directors to dispense with borrowing any portion of the proposed capital. The bill was presented to the House of Commons on 3 February 1844, passed through Committee and finally obtained the Royal Assent on 7 June 1844.[16]

The 'Act for making a Railway from the Lancaster and Preston Junction Railway to, or near to, the City of Carlisle of 1844'[17] authorised the raising of the sum of £900,000 in shares, with powers to raise an additional £300,000 in loans.[18] The Company decided that this sum should be used so as to lay a double line. Of the 12 directors 6 were nominees of the Railway Companies. The landed gentry of Cumberland and Westmorland provided 4 directors and John Dixon and G. H. Head occupied the remaining vacancies. Joseph Locke was appointed as Engineer in chief, and J. E. Errington the resident engineer with Messrs Worthington and Larmer his assistants. The contractors appointed were Messrs John Stephenson, Brassey and MacKenzie.

A provisional agreement with the contractors enabled work to commence shortly after the Royal Assent.[19] The line presented a major challenge. It was alleged in some quarters that a locomotive on a smooth rail could not ascend the maximum gradient of 1 in 75 on Shap; that the route would be closed in winter because of the snow at the altitude of the Shap summit and 'King' Hudson the east coast railway magnate was reported as saying that half the year the line would be covered with snow, and rather irrelevantly dismissed the scheme as a 'wild-goose chase' over the moors, ten miles of which would not support a goose.[20] The engineer and the contractors had no such qualms. The first sod was cut on Shap Fells on 18 July 1844, on 18 November the

Joseph Locke. Engineer-in-Chief, Lancaster and Carlsile Railway.

first permanent rail was laid in the same locality and shortly afterwards 2,500 men were at work upon the line. At the peak of construction 10,000 were employed and throughout the project the average number of men working was 5,000.[21]

The accommodation of the work force along the line was one of the problems that had to be faced. On Shap summit, the Journal reported:

> There being no houses within a reasonable distance of this wild and bleak region, a colony of mud huts was erected for the use of the 'navvies' and attached to them were a church and a school – built by the enterprising contractors, who also paid the salaries of the minister and schoolmaster . . . Though the material of which they were composed cannot be praised for its beauty, it answered every purpose, and formed comfortable dwellings for about 500 workmen – the roofs being thatched and the floors boarded. The various rows being christened by the 'navvies' after the names of the most celebrated streets in London – such as 'Regent St', 'Hanover Square' etc.[22]

The Journal's picture verges on the idyllic, but it is in stark contrast to that given by the Rev. J. Gillie who was employed as a chaplain to tend to the spiritual and moral needs of the railway labourers on the Lancaster to Carlisle Railway. He was called upon to give evidence to the Select Committee of Railway Labourers (House of Commons Parliamentary Papers 1846 vol. 13 pp. 162–7) and was asked what was the nature of the huts in which the men lived. He disclosed:

> They are mostly constructed of mud; it is turf cut from the grass; these turfs piled above each other to about 4½ ft. to 5 ft. in height, and then there are small sticks laid in the way of rafters and these are covered with straw.

The huts, Gillie reported, were constructed by the contractor, 14ft. wide and 42ft. long and divided into 2 compartments; one compartment was reserved for meals and the other for sleeping. They were individually let to a man and a woman, who took in lodgers. Up to 19 men and women could be housed in one hut. The rent for the hut was initially set at 2s per week but then reduced to 1s. When labour became scarce they were let free to encourage men to stay on the scheme.

The challenge presented by this 70 mile stretch of line, in the days before the advent of earth moving machinery, was immense. The excavations averaged 100,000 cubic yards per mile, and as Stephenson reported to the directors one sixth of the excavations had turned out to be trap rock, and constituted formidable uncalculated expense. 200 tons of gunpowder had been used on the rock and on the '400,000 yards of samel' (sic) that required blasting, 'as being so hard a material could not be overcome by any other means than gunpowder'.[23]

The peak labour force of 10,000 men employed 930 horses[24] and used 2,500 wagons and 3,500 wheelbarrows. In addition to earth moving the constructional work involved the building of 5 viaducts and 219 bridges. Because of the great demand for labour the average wage of a labourer quickly rose from 2s. 6d. per day at the commencement of the scheme to 3s. 6d. per day.[25]

The complete work was finished in 2 years 5 months at a cost per mile, for the double line, of £17,000; inside the cost estimate, and only a little outside the time estimate of 2 years in spite of the scheme revision to a double line, the unexpected amount of rock excavation, and more critically the delay in getting possession of some of the land. The line was opened on 15 December 1846 and Carlisle people, as is their wont on great occasions, went on a general holiday. In an incisive reply to the cynics, the first train with 200 passengers ascended the steepest gradient on Shap, 1 in 75, in the depth of winter, at a speed of 22 mph.[26]

Edward William Hassell who was appointed first chairman of the Lancaster-Carlisle railway had his seat at Dalemain appropriately close to the fine viaduct across the R. Eamont.

Carlisle now had a direct rail link with London and the connection to Glasgow was soon to follow. The Caledonian Co., with the same engineers Locke and Errington and the same contractors Messrs Stephenson, Brassey and MacKenzie opened the first section of their line from Carlisle to Beattock summit on 10 September 1847 when a train left Citadel Station for Beattock.[27] The west coast route to Glasgow was completed on 15 February 1848, over 2 years before the rival east coast route London to Edinburgh.

The completion of the Lancaster and Carlisle railway was celebrated by a director's dinner at the Athenaeum, and/a contractors dinner at the Crown and Mitre Coffee House. These were splendid occasions when congratulations passed between directors and shareholders and tributes were paid to the truly outstanding engineers and contractors employed on this enterprise. The obverse of the great technological achievements of the Victorian engineers was the exploitation and degradation of masses of illiterate and inarticulate men whose only assets were muscle and endurance. It is to the 10,000 excavators, or navvies, who carried out this work, often in appalling conditions, in an incredibly short time, that attention will now be directed. The 'navigators' have been variously described in tones of black or white. First, a sympathetic description by Samuel Smiles of a striking man portrayed con brio

He usually wore a white felt hat with the brim turned up, a velveteen or jean square-tailed coat, a scarlet plush waistcoat with little black spots, and a bright-coloured kerchief round his herculean neck, when, as often happened, it was not left entirely bare. His corduroy breeches were retained in position by a leather strap round the waist, and were tied and buttoned at the knee, displaying beneath a solid calf and foot encased in strong high-laced boots . . . Their powers of endurance were extraordinary. In times of emergency, they would work for 12 or even 16 hours, with only short intervals for meals. The quantity of flesh-meat which they consumed was something enormous; but it was to their bones and muscles what coke is to the locomotive – the means of keeping up the steam.[28]

Next, a portrait of the same men but drawn from a different angle. Robert Rawlinson in a paper to Edwin Chadwick wrote:

. . . no man cares for them, they labour like degraded brutes; they feed and lodge like savages; they are enveloped in vice as earth with an atmosphere.[29]

The gathering together of a vast workforce of 10,000 men and deploying them in a sparsely populated countryside, with no more preparation for their accommodation than that for an army on active service, was to cause grave problems. The Report of the Select Committee in July 1846 was a very belated recognition of a problem that could have been predicted. The Committee concluded that the work forces

. . . are brought hastily together in large bodies; no time is given for that gradual growth of accommodation which would naturally accompany the gradual growth in numbers, they are therefore crowded into unwholesome dwellings, while scarcely any provision is made for their comfort or decency of living; they are released from the useful influence of domestic ties, and the habits of their former routine of life; they are hard worked; they are exposed to great risk of life and limb; they are too often harshly treated; and many inducements are presented to them to be thoughtless, thriftless and improvident.[30]

Under these conditions the Committee concluded

. . . that intemperance, disorder and demoralisation run a better chance than decency, frugality and improvement, and they cannot wonder at the feelings of dislike, and dismay, with which the permanent inhabitants of a neighbourhood often view the arrival of strangers among them.[31]

The Committee's Report, and warning, did no more than describe what was currently happening on the Lancaster-Carlisle line. Brassey's agent MacKay spoke of 'Beer given to the men as well as wages. Lookouts on the road to intercept men tramping – work night and day. Provisions dear, excessively high wages, excessive work, excessive drinking, indifferent lodgings caused great demoralisation.'[32]

The payment of wages at intervals of a month, rather than weekly, the provision of credit, at exorbitant interest rates, the evils of the truck system of payment of wages in kind from monopoly shops were means of exploitation and a snare to the improvident workman. Men were soon in debt and the next pay day did not help when the navvies spent their wages immediately on alcohol.[33] It was on pay day that riots and disorder were triggered off. The files of the Westmorland Gazette for the years 1844–46 record many incidents of violence, and the Chaplain of Appleby Gaol reported:

> Nearly half of those who have been inmates of the prison have been entire strangers. No fewer than 26 of those that have been committed have been labourers from the lines of Railway which are now being made through the county.
>
> Perhaps I ought also to state, that several of these men have expressed to me an opinion that if their wages were paid weekly, or at shorter intervals than those at present in use, the disgusting scenes, and the evil consequences which arise from monthly payments, might in a great measure be prevented.[34]

The fact that the labour force was made up of contingents of English, Scottish and Irish labourers caused its own problems. They were normally segregated and worked on separate sections of the line but when they clashed, especially if it was a pay night, the consequences for civil peace were disastrous. The most notorious incident led to the Penrith riots of 11 February 1846. The sequence of events with marches and countermarches was recorded in the Journal. It started with a fracas between an Irish labourer and a ganger at a railway cutting south of Penrith. The remaining Irish, 60 in number, out of the total local work force of 660, went to Plumpton to join up with the 500 Irish employed there. The combined Irish force marched through Penrith to the huts in Yanwath Moor intending to burn them down but were stopped by the magistrates and civil powers. The next day 2,000 railway labourers employed between Kendal and Penrith assembled at Penrith with a view to driving the Irish from the Line, but by then the main body of the Irish had retreated but left behind some Irish who took refuge in a common lodging house. The mob broke in 'and assaulted 9 Irishmen and one or two left for dead' before order was restored by the Cumberland and Westmorland Yeomanry. The next day the Irishmen to the number of between 2 and 3 hundred, armed with guns and other warlike weapons, were met by the Yeomanry Cavalry at Milestone House and stopped, but eventually they laid down their arms, were paid off and left the town.[35] The geography of these events is: Plumpton is a few miles north, and Yanwath a few miles south, of Penrith.

By the end of 1848 Carlisle had important rail connections to London, Glasgow and Edinburgh, and by the mid century the great centres of population of the country were connected together by great arterial lines. A high price had been paid in human degradation of massive unskilled work forces, but the rewards were immense, truly on a revolutionary scale as the economic and social life of the country was transformed. Industry was given the opportunity to develop mass markets on a scale not possible with road and canal transport, and the railways themselves became a great industry in their own right, particularly so in Carlisle. What however had not been recognised in the early days was the enormous potential of passenger traffic from all sections of the community. For people of adequate means the whole country was open to them in a way that was unthinkable in stage coach days. Even the skilled artisan, and workman, could share in the great travel boom albeit with some, but not unaccustomed, discomfort. Gladstone's Railway Act of 1844 ordained that on each line, one train per day in each direction, should carry third class passengers at 1d per mile (i.e. the old penny ¹/₂₄₀ of a pound), and stop at each station. While the 'parliamentary trains', as they were dubbed, were notorious for their slowness and inconvenience, they did successfully tap the bottom end of the market. The early third class carriages on the Newcastle and Carlisle line, as shown on the Carmichael print, were hardly better than open cattle trucks, but they were improved to become the covered carriages on the parliamentary trains. Higher in the social scale of this class conscious society the second class passenger could travel in a covered upholstered carriage befitting his superior status in society, while the gentry would travel first class in considerable style. The rapidity of long distance travel was something that could not be dreamed about in stage coach days; average speeds for a journey could be in excess of 30 m. p. h. and the whole country was being opened up to even the less intrepid traveller. Thackeray's observations on the transformation in the life of the country in the railway age has been noted; Elizabeth Gaskell complements this with an account of the effect of this strange form of transport on a sensitive traveller. Mary Barton, travelling between Manchester and Liverpool in the 1840s, had been overwhelmed by a sense of wonder.

> Mary had never been on one before, and she felt bewildered by the hurry, the noise of people and bells, and horns, the whiz and scream of arriving trains.[36]

But there were more subtle ways in which the new mode of transport was effecting the lives of the people. The railways brought about the standardisation of times; where previously there had been a great deal of local variation throughout the country. In the 1850s cities were keeping London time, checked each day with the watch carried by the guard. In the same period first steps were taken in a communication revolution. The establishment of rail routes provided a clear channel on which electric telegraph cables could be laid and there was a rapid growth in the service after 1846. Of even greater significance for people in general was the inauguration of the 'penny post' by Rowland Hill in 1840 when mail was carried to all parts of the United Kingdom at a standard charge of one penny, whereas previously mail by coach was expensive with postage varying according to distance. It was the extension of the rail network that made this a viable proposition to the great advantage of the public.

The negative side of the transport revolution was the damage caused by railways to some vested interests. The long distance coaches had virtually been knocked out by 1850 and with their demise the traditional posting inns fell upon hard times. But there was a negative reaction of much greater concern for some of the industrialist and business men who had done so much to bring Carlisle into the new era. A cautionary tale must now be told in more detail of the entrepreneurs who had constructed the Carlisle Canal to get the industrialist out of the straight jacket of transport constraints but now, with rail competition, found themselves in financial difficulties. Mention has already been made of their growing unease, after the first euphoric years following the opening of the Newcastle and Carlisle railway; first of all when the Carlisle and Maryport line was opened which was followed within a few years by the greater threat of the north-south railway trunk routes. The directors of the Canal Co., unwillingly drawn into the big financial world which they had no power to control, now resorted to more and more desperate expedients which after early successes turned into financial disasters. Finally they were drawn into an audacious speculation, the construction of a new town and the development of a holiday industry which was remote from their industrial and commercial experience. The irony of the situation was that the development of the national railway network, which brought disaster upon many of Carlisle's pioneering entrepreneurs, was finally to lead to a more prosperous and better balanced city. The affairs of the Carlisle Canal Co., after mid century, the Carlisle-Port Carlisle railway and the Silloth Railway Co., must now receive our attention.

The position of the Carlisle Canal in the early railway age was ambivalent and a distinction can be drawn between its profitability and its importance on a commercial link; not least for the Carlisle industrialist. The *Carlisle Journal* in 1858 could write:

> For thirty years past a great part of the traffic between Liverpool and Newcastle has been by way of the Solway and Carlisle. Before the construction of the Newcastle and Carlisle railway it was brought to Carlisle by canal, and thence carted by carriers to Newcastle. Since railways have been made, they have, of course, played a large part in conducting it; but in the years 1851 and 1852, according to the evidence of the present manager of the Newcastle and Carlisle Railway, more than one-half of the whole traffic between Liverpool and Newcastle came by way of Port Carlisle. The other half went by York, and was delivered in Newcastle by the North-Eastern.[37]

In financial terms the outlook in the late 1840s was not so optimistic. Walton produces evidence that the Canal Co. was in some financial difficulty and the last dividend that had been paid was in 1848.[38] The development of the railway network in England, with the greatly increased speed of transit and the volume of goods that could be carried, combined with ruthless competition between railway companies, was soon to render Port Carlisle, with its dependence upon tides and restricted harbour facilities, obsolete. The conversion of the canal to a railway, by filling in the canal and building the railway on the same course, was a doomed venture, and it was soon to be incorporated into a larger and more ambitious scheme.

The line to Prot Carlisle was opened in 1854 but already the construction of an alternative port in Silloth Bay which had 'formed a topic of public discussion for many years'[39] was being energetically considered. The Mayor of Carlisle Mr P. J. Dixon convened a meeting in July 1853 which was attended by leading citizens, including local cotton magnates and by Mr J. D. Carr, who was to play a prominent role in subsequent industrial and commercial development at Silloth. The ad hoc Committee called upon expert advice from Mr Geddes, the superintendent of the lighting and buoying of the Solway Firth, Captain Logan, and proxy evidence was taken from Captains Robinson and Beechy of the Royal Navy.

In the early days, before the project became bedeviled by railway politics, the merits of a new harbour at Silloth were compelling. The basic requirement was that the port should be accessible in all weathers with minimal delay due to tides. The expert advice given to the Committee was that vessels could ride safely in Silloth Bay at any time of tide, at any time of night and in the highest wind. Vessels could arrive and depart at all hours, and if docks were constructed vessels could dock at 2 hours flood and have 6 hours to work upon before departing. Compared with other ports in the Solway there were major advantages. For Port Carlisle navigation up the channel from Silloth Bay was difficult. A steamer could land passengers 3 to 4 hours sooner at Silloth than at Prot Carlisle and no time would be wasted waiting for high water at the latter port. Compared with Maryport the Committee was advised that it was as easy for vessels of 1000 tons to get in as it was for vessels of 500 tons at Maryport.

For many passengers, a harbour at Silloth, in conjunction with the railway network, would offer considerable advantage for travellers to and from Ireland with shorter combined steamer or rail times. For Carlisle passengers the advantages were obvious, Dublin could be reached by way of Silloth in 11 hours whereas it would take 15½ hours by way of Liverpool and 14 hours by way of Holyhead, a saving of 4½ hours and 3 hours respectively. The remaining criterion to be met for the operation of a successful port, the cooperation of the railway companies, seemed, at this early stage to be certain. The Committee reassured by the favourable response from the Newcastle and Carlisle Co., and from the Chairman of the Hawick line to the Silloth proposal, enthusiastically supported the project.[40] Authority was sought to promote the Carlisle and Silloth Bay Railway and Dock Co., the first bill of 1854 met with strong opposition and was rejected, but the second application in 1855 received parliamentary approval.[41]

The Carlisle and Silloth Bay railway had almost unanimous support from Carlisle's leading citizens of whom 201, of the 245 shareholders, accounted for £94,000 of the £112,000 subscribed. Subscribers included 29 Carlisle city councillors, ten mayors of the city, important cotton industrialists such as the Dixon and Ferguson families, and J. D. Carr the biscuit and flour industrialist.[42] The line over flat terrain presented no problems, being only 12 miles from its junction with the Carlisle–Port Carlisle line at Drumburgh, itself 9 miles from Carlisle, to the sea at Silloth Bay. The *Carlisle Journal* of 29 August 1856 reported on

> the virtual completion of this important work – a fresh link in a chain of communication between the German and Atlantic Oceans, – uniting New-castle-upon-Tyne with a harbour on the Solway, as yet only partially constructed – was celebrated yesterday.[43]

As with the opening of the canal, a third of a century earlier, it was an occasion of great celebrations. Businesses closed down for the day and 'the swarming population of Caldewgate seemed to have taken a holiday'.[44] Despite foul weather in the morning a 'train of enormous length', and a relief train, carried many of the 3,000 people who witnessed the opening ceremony for the line.

The tone of the 1857 summer meeting, one year after the opening of the railway, was optimistic and self-congratulatory. The Chairman, Mr. P. J. Dixon, said the report

> Was highly satisfactory; and he was glad to congratulate the shareholders upon the fact that the prospects of the undertaking were gradually improv-ing, and that the most sanguine expectations would probably soon be realised.[45]

The traffic was admittedly only local as the work on the dock had just started[46] but the pier was available for the shipping and discharging of cargoes, and the steamer Silloth, plying between Silloth and Liverpool, had been making use of it for the last 4 months. It was anticipated that in 3 or 4 months a steamer would ply between Silloth and Belfast and Dublin.[47]

The directors were anxious that the port should be opened up to the national railway network. In 1853 the Calidonian Co., who had a close working relationship with the Carlisle–Lancaster Railway Co., had failed to obtain parliamentary approval for a connecting line to the Carlisle and Silloth railway because the House of Commons Committee considered that the proposal did not give facilities for the traffic of the district.[48] This opinion was shared by the directors of the Carlisle and Silloth Co., who had strong suspicions, to be confirmed in later years, that discriminatory freight charges would siphon off traffic from the Silloth to Liverpool route. The directors expressed a strong preference for an arrangement with the North British Railway Co., who wished to connect Hawick with Carlisle so as to give an outlet ot the sea at Silloth for their mineral and passenger traffic. For the Carlisle and Silloth Co., this gave mutual advantage. It would give access to Edinburgh, the Scottish border towns, and to two ports Leith and Berwick facing the continent.

Pending the completion of the dock the Committee, seeking other means to obtain revenue to meet interest charges, built up passenger traffic from Carlisle with great success. During July and August 1857 the number of passengers using the railway to Silloth averaged 1,450 per week. Concurrently the company attempted to build up a holiday resort. They purchased common land, consisting of little more than sandhills and rabbit warrens, laid out a street network and started selling building plots; in effect to create a new town to the north of the railway and docks. But this was not the limit of their bounding ambition: during the first half of 1857 they purchased the remainder of Blitterlees Common, amounting to 140 acres to the south of the dock to give a total sea frontage of 2 miles, to permit the extension of the town and to allow space for industrial development.[49]

The optimism of the August 1857 report was soon found to be premature; concurrently an ominous development was taking place in railway politics.

The Newcastle and Carlisle Railway Co. agreed with the North-Eastern Railway Co. to divert the lucrative traffic from the north-east to Liverpool and Ireland via a southerly route through Yorkshire and Lancashire to Liverpool. The Port Carlisle and the Silloth Railway Companies submitted a memorial to a Parliamentary Committee protesting against this interference with the free flow of trade and accusing the N. E. Co. and the N. & C. Co. of establishing a monopoly against the public interest.

The memorialist claimed that in 1856 the N. & C. Co. had entered into an agreement with the N. E. Co. to divert the Newcastle-Liverpool traffic on to a longer route of 192 miles through York and Normanton to Liverpool. To make their plan effective the N. & C. Co. would pay the N. E. Co. 13s 4d for every ton, for Liverpool, carried on the Carlisle line: an amount higher than the full local rate for this line. In compensation the N. E. Co. would pay the N. & C. Co. 6s 1d per ton upon one third of tonnage carried on their line between Newcastle and Liverpool.

The effect of this was intended to close the N. & C. railway for all Liverpool traffic and to compel the public to make use of a longer and more expensive route.[50] The measures were entirely effective, the Liverpool traffic over the N. & C. line ceased in April 1857 and the rates for certain classes of goods increased by 50% as the result of the monopoly of carriage.[51]

This strange, quiet, acceptance by the L. N. & W. Co. of the diversion of the Liverpool-Newcastle traffic from the west to the east coast confirms the suspicious that the Carlisle directors had long entertained when they considered whether to link up with the N. B. Co. or the Caledonian.

Meanwhile the directors' efforts were directed to the creation of a new town, and the results were impressive. The street pattern of the town had been laid out, the roads paved and footpaths flagged. Speculative builders, under close supervision to maintain standards, were erecting houses, while the directors, wishing to erect a superior type of building on the main street (Criffel St), were erecting the terrace themselves and this work was almost complete.[52] They were also engaged in major landscaping by levelling the sandhills between Criffel St. and the Solway and laying turf to form 'the Green' at a cost of £6,000. The directors were enthusiastic about Silloth's 'great capabilities and advantages as a watering place' and wished to develop the town as quickly as possible. They announced a new Family Hotel would be opened in a few days and they anticipated the completion of the gas works by October primarily to light the dock area to permit loading at night, but also to light the streets of the town.[53]

The town was thriving resort in August 1860 with 4 hotels and 38 lodging houses. A local weekly newspaper, the Silloth Gazette, first published in the summer of 1860, lists the visitors staying in the resort. The list is impressive, apart from local holiday makers, there were numerous visitors from locations as far apart as London and Edinburgh; visitors from New York, and members of the landed aristocracy in the persons of Lord Scarsdale of Kedleston Hall and, presumably the related Curzons, from Derby.[54]

The establishment of a thriving resort, rapidly gaining renown, within 4 years of its inception, was a remarkable achievement, but it resulted from an unauthorised venture, of dubious legality, by a company close to bankruptcy. While precedents had been set for the creation of Victorian resorts, the appearance of Silloth with its orderly and spacious layout, its broad streets, and well built and properly sewered houses, and its fine landscaped open space (the 'Green') between town and sea, was in dramatic contrast with the congestion and squalor still present in contemporary (i.e. 1860s) Carlisle. What is surprising on comparing the street maps of 1860, and the amenities, shops, hotels listed in the Gazette,[55] with present day Silloth is that the town has remained essentially unaltered, except for the loss of the pier, for the last 130 years; a fascinating bonus for the historian but no doubt disappointing to others.

Silloth was closely identified with Carlisle and became the city's place of recreation, at least before the days of conspicuous travel of the post World War 2 era. With two pierrot companies, cinema and adventurist golf course, it satisfied the pre-war holiday makers. The modern, more demanding, holiday maker evidently requires more than the spacious tranquillity of Silloth, with its invigorating climate and spectacular sunsets over Criffel.

The new dock was opened in August 1859. The North British scheme for a connection with the Carlisle and Silloth railway gained parliamentary approval in the same year but it was not until 1862 that traffic began to flow to Silloth's new dock. The summer meetings of the Carlisle and Silloth Co. and the Port Carlisle Railway Co. in 1861 were sombre. The Chairman of the former Co. maintained that traffic, both passenger and goods, on the line had increased satisfactorily, and vessels of large burthen could enter the docks, but 'they had facilities for carrying on a much larger traffic than they unfortunately had at present', but he was confident that 'when the Border Union line was open, and the North British line fully developed, the facilities they had here would commend a large and important traffic, and in the end be remunerative as they had every reason to expect.' 'Let their motto be Nil desperandum'.[56]

The Company had introduced cheap passenger fares to Silloth to boost revenue, but this did not please at least one of the influential directors of the Port Carlisle Co. Mr Joseph Ferguson

> thought the cheap trains were a downright nuisance. He had not gone down to Silloth since they had started, nor did he intend to go. People did not like to go down every day like that, with the mob. It was neither pleasant nor safe to do so.[57]

Clearly a two nation culture still persisted regardless of this complaint there was a price induced, class segregation on the trains. The 1857 Report revealed that in the half year ending in 12 June, 542 second class passengers had travelled at an average cost of $7\frac{1}{2}$ d. each, while the 1002 first class passengers paid nearly double, i.e. 1s. 3d.[58]

The suspicions that had been long entertained about collusion between the N. E. Co. and the West Coast railways was confirmed when the *Cumberland Pacquet* of 27 May 1862 announced the terms under which the L. N. W. Railway Co. abandoned opposition to the N. E. Co. and Newcastle and Carlisle Co. amalgamation in return for (i) the N. E. Co. affords facilities for through booking from Newcastle to Liverpool via the L. & C. Railway, (ii) the N. E. Co. to pay the L. & N. W. £1,000 p. a. for use of the Citadel station and £250 p.a. for management expenses. From this time the use of the London Road station in Carlisle for passengers was discontinued.

The Carlisle and Silloth Railway and Dock Co., and the Port Carlisle Railway Co. were rescued from their untenable financial position when they were taken over by the North British Railway Co. in 1862. The directors admitted, in their February 1861 Report, that the capital which the company had been authorised/to raise by shares and debentures had been greatly exceeded. The Company's share capital was £165,000 and they had been empowered to borrow £55,000.[59] £100,000 of this share capital had been provided by the directors. The amount actually expended on railway, docks, and in the creation of the town, amounted to £290,000, and the extra amount had been borrowed by the directors on personal guarantees. To pay off the debt, and to complete minor works, nearly £100,000 of extra capital was required.[60] The bill promoted for the leasing of the Silloth Co. to the N. B. Co. was to permit the N. B. Co. to pay interest on the £165,000, and in addition the N. B. Co. would pay the Silloth Co. £2,000 annual rent.

Lord Redesdale, Chairman of the Committee on Parliamentary Private Bills clearly looked upon the proposals as exceedingly generous to the Silloth and Port Carlisle Companies, and his comments were scathing. The terse exchanges between Lord Redesdale and Mr Nanson, solicitor to the Silloth Co. in May 1862, left little doubt that the companies were fortunate to be allowed to extricate themselves from the financial morass into which they had sunk.

For Bill No. 1, the leasing of the Silloth Co. to the N. B. Co. the exchanges were reported as follows:

Lord Redesdale	How long have the Silloth Railway and Dock been open?
Mr Nanson	A little more than 2 years.
L. R.	What dividend do the company pay?
N.	Not any.
L. R.	Are the North British shareholders to give you £2,000 p. a. for nothing?
N.	They hope to make the undertaking pay.
L. R.	It looks like insanity, you must insert a clause in the bill . . . to save the holders of preference shares in the N. B. Co. from injury.

and so the bill passed.

For the bill for the raising of another £100,000 in capital to pay off the amount expended by the Company in excess of their previous authorization, the verbal exchanges were

Lord Redesdale	What sum do you seek to raise by preference shares?
Mr Nanson	£75,000.
L. R.	And you want to borrow £15,000 in addition?
N.	Yes
L. R.	What do you want all this money for?
N.	To pay off our debt.
L. R.	Oh, wretched, wretched. You begin by spending your money in the erection of a town at Silloth in order to create traffic for your railway and dock. – How can you hope ever to repay £90,000, or the interest on that sum, out of £2,000 a year? You admit the railway and dock have not produced a dividend, and yet you seek to add

£90,000 to your existing liabilities and engagements. I
don't see my way to pass the bill at all. I confess I do
not. But however if the N. B. Co. are so infatuated with
your wretched scheme they had better take it. – Who
do you think will ever lend you a penny on such a rot-
ten and ruined concern as this, in fact, appears unques-
tionably to be.

Lord Redesdale was equally harsh in commentating on the Bill for the leasing
of the Port Carlisle Co. to the N. B. Co.; with the transfer of debts and liabilities;
and leaving to the Port Carlisle Co. only their original capital.

The parliamentary correspondent of the Carlisle Patriot summed up

. . . the bill was allowed finally to pass. It, however, at one time appeared
very doubtful whether his lordship would sanction it. All the three bills,
although unopposed, had a narrow escape. They just succeeded in getting
through, and no more.[61]

But the very fact the, presumably hard headed, business men of the N. B. Railway Co., not given to throwing their money away, were prepared to take
over the Silloth and Port Carlisle Companies on these terms, suggests that Lord
Redesdale was perhaps taking a narrow financial view of the position. It was
a vital N. B. Co. requirement that they should break out of their straight-jacket
and connect up with the west coast and Ireland. Silloth, admittedly, had not
been viable without its Newcastle link, but the N. B. Co. gave it an alternative
east coast connection and opened it up to the Scottish border towns and
Edinburgh.

The Silloth Bay Co. passed into the hands of the N. B. Co. on the 16 June
1862, on the day that the through route to Hawick was opened. From this
date the N. B. Co. were able to work the whole route Edinburgh to Silloth
as one line.[62]

The Silloth line remained viable until after the second World War when,
unable to compete with the rapid growth of road transport, goods and private
cars, it fell under the Beeching axe in 1963.

As regards the Carlisle industrialists who had invested large sums in these
ill-starred ventures to ensure reliable communication with the port of Liverpool,
and the cotton markets of Manchester, they were rescued from their grave
financial predicament by another twist of railway intrigue and opportunism,
but they lost their independent communication with Liverpool and from
henceforth they had to depend upon identity of interests with the L.N.W.
Railway Co.

The Settle to Carlisle Railway

The last great railway project undertaken in the Victorian era was the Settle to Carlisle line. Although a triumph of engineering and a spectacular route it was of dubious financial viability. The railway had an inauspicious birth. During the 1860s, in the second railway boom, the Midland Company sought to compete with their great rivals, the L. N. W. R. and the L. N. E. R., for the lucrative Scottish traffic. Their line reached only as far north as Ingleton and after failure to reach agreement with the L. N. W. R. for the joint use of the line from Lancaster to Carlisle, they decided to extend their own line to Carlisle. In July 1866 the Settle-Carlisle Railway Bill was approved by parliament, and work started in September. This stopped at the end of December for almost two years, because of financial difficulties, but joint use of the Lancaster to Carlisle line was agreed. An application to parliament for an abandonment bill in April 1870 was refused, and work on the Settle line began. The project with its 72 miles of track, 17 viaducts, 12 tunnels and innumerable cuttings and embankments was a triumph for the engineer but a financial gamble for the company. It took six and a half years to complete, and cost £3½m., the labour force peaking at 6,000 men. Express trains were running to Carlisle, and then to Glasgow via the Glasgow and S. W. Scotland Co., and to Edinburgh via the N. B. R. C. by 1876.

The efforts of the Carlisle industrialists to safeguard their trade routes had not turned out as planned, but the city's development as a major rail centre was to be of prime importance in ensuring the city's industrial future. This was acknowledged by the *Carlisle Guide* of 1881:

There are few towns which have more largely shared in the national prosperity resulting from the development of the railway system that Carlisle . . . It is an undoubted fact that the last 10 or 15 years have been more productive of material progress than any previous period of the same length – if not, indeed, of the half century. There were certainly never so many streets laid out, or houses built, or manufactories erected, or improvements made, as in the time denoted. Railways gave the impetus to these strides of prosperity, which have gone on contemporaneously with the prosperity of the system that called them into existence. Carlisle is now a great centre of railway communication. East, West, North, South the iron roads radiate from it. It is placed on two of the three great trunk lines which run from one end of the kingdom to the other, and has short and easy access to the eastern and western seas.[63]

A visible symbol of the importance of the railways to Carlisle is the dignified citadel station, designed by Sir William Tite in the Tudor style, and built 1847–8. In the early days each railway company in Carlisle had its own station, viz the Carlisle-Newcastle on London Rd, the Carlisle-Maryport at Crown St, the Silloth line at the Canal basin and the London and North Western and the Caledonian at the citadel station. This station was built at the expense of these last two companies and to it the various other companies were gradually admitted.[64] Rail traffic increased dramatically and by 1870 as many as 138 passenger trains were arriving and departing from the station every 24 hours.[65] But in addition to this an enormous through goods traffic had to be passed through the station each day. This was both inconvenient and dangerous and an act was obtained in 1873 to permit the goods traffic to be separated from the passenger traffic by diverting it to the West of the station, between the inner city and the Denton Holme and Caldewgate suburbs. The passenger station was enlarged in 1873–6 and in place of the old single platforms and a couple of bays there were three platforms of great length for working the passenger traffic north and south, and some half dozen bays to accommodate the traffic that terminates in Carlisle. The station was run by a joint-stock undertaking whose shareholders were the individual railway companies viz L. & N. W., Caledonian, Midland, North British, L. N. E. and Glasgow and South-Western. The Carlisle and Maryport Co. was accommodated but only as tenants.[66] The Citadel station at the end of the nineteenth century provided a magnificent spectacle that one can hardly hope to be repeated. The majestic steam engines of the 7 different railway companies, each company with its distinctively coloured livery for locomotives and rolling stock, and the splendid figure of the station master with his top hat and frock coat, a more exulted descendent of the guards dressed in gold-laced scarlet coats and white hats who had conducted the passengers to their coaches at the terminus of the N. & C. railway.[67] The anonymity of the modern station can no longer provide the sense of occasion of the citadel station of a century ago.

NOTES

1. W. M. Thackeray, 'De Juventate' from *Cornhill Magazine* (1860).
2. W. Chapman, *Report on Advantages of Canal or Railway Newcastle to Carlisle* (1824).
3. 10 Geo. IV c. 72.
4. e.g. Stationary steam engines for hauling wagons up steep gradients.
5. Mannix and Whellan, *History, Gazetteer and Directory of Cumberland* (1847), p. 40.
6. C. Hadfield & G. Biddle, *Canals of N. W. England*, vol. 2, p. 343.
7. S. Jefferson, *History and Antiquities of Carlisle* (1838), pp. 305–7.
8. Mannix and Whellan, op. cit., p. 145.
9. 1 Vic. c. 101.
10. The North Union resulted from the merger of the Newton–Wigan, and Wigan–Preston railways.
11. *Carlisle Journal*, 18 December 1846.
12. Ibid.

13. Ibid.

14. Ibid.

15. Ibid.

16. Ibid.

17. 7 Vic. c. 37 6.6.1844.

18. The Grand Junction Co. subscribed £250,000, the London & Birmingham Co. £100,000, the North Union Co. £65,000 and the Lancaster and Preston Co. £65,000.

19. *Carlisle Journal*, 18 December 1846.

20. Ibid.

21. Ibid.

22. Ibid.

23. Ibid.

24. The *Carlisle Journal* gave the figure of 930 horses, but Mr Mould, Superintendent for the contractors, was reported as saying that 10,500 horses were employed. Possibly this referred to the whole period of the contract, but if the figures are to be reconciled the inference must be that there was a horrific wastage of horses.

25. *Carlisle Journal*, 18 December 1846.

26. Ibid.

27. *Carlisle Journal*, 11 September 1847.

28. Samuel Smiles *Lives of the Engineers*. George & Robert Stephenson. New edition John Murray (1879) pp. 250–1.

29. Paper by Robert Rawlinson read before the Statistical Society of Manchester on the *Demoralisation and Injuries occasioned by the want of proper regulations of Labourers engaged in Construction and Working of Railways* p. 49.

30. *Report from the Select Committed on Railway Labourers* 28 July 1846.

31. Ibid.

32. Jack Gould, *Thomas Brassey*, p. 18.

33. Report from Select Committee, op. cit.

34. Ibid.

35. *Carlisle Journal*, 13 February 1846.

36. Elizabeth Gaskell, *Mary Barton* (Penguin, 1982), p. 343.

37. *Carlisle Journal*, 17 December 1858.

38. Dr J. K. Walton, *Railways and Resort Development in Victorian England. The Case of Silloth*, Northern History (1979), p. 196.

39. *Carlisle Journal*, 29 July 1853.

40. Ibid.

41. 18 & 19 Vic. c. 153 (1855).

42. Walton, op. cit. The history of the Carlisle and Silloth Railway Co. has been finely researched by Dr John Walton. I have made use of his references for much of my source material.

43. *Carlisle Journal*, 29 August 1856.

44. Ibid.

45. *Carlisle Journal*, 21 August 1857.

46. The foundation stone of this dock was laid by Sir James Graham, MP for Carlisle and formerly First Lord of the Admiralty.

47. *Carlisle Journal,* 21 August 1857.

48. Ibid.

49. Ibid.

50. *Carlisle Journal,* 17 December 1858.

51. Ibid.

52. Ibid.

53. Ibid.

54. *Silloth Gazette,* 4 and 11 August 1860.

55. Ibid.

56. *Carlisle Journal,* 30 August 1861.

57. Ibid.

58. *Carlisle Journal,* 21 August 1857.

59. The Act of 1855 (18 & 19 Vic. c. 153) authorised a share capital for the railway and harbour of £165,000. The Company was also empowered to borrow money to a total of £55,000 for the railway and dock. In both cases the expenditure was authorised only for the purpose laid down in the Act, i.e. Railway and dock. No authority was given for expenditure on creating a new town.

60. *Carlisle Journal,* 28 February 1861.

61. *Carlisle Patriot,* 27 May 1862.

62. *Carlisle Journal,* 29 August 1862.

63. *Guide to Carlisle* (1881), pp. 136–7.

64. T. Bulmer, *Directory of East Cumberland* (1884), p. 57.

65. John M. Howard, *Notes on the Railways of Carlisle* (Tullie House Museum Carlisle).

66. Bulmer, loc. cit.

67. R. S. Ferguson, *History of Cumberland* (1890), pp. 279–80. The first travellers on this railway were not supplied with tickets but their names were booked on a way bill.

CHAPTER 8

The Mature Victorian City

A study of the development of Carlisle, in the century and a quarter after the Jacobite rebellion, has afforded a unique opportunity to observe the transition of an essentially medieval society to a thriving industrial community. Carlisle in 1745 was a beleaguered fortified city, a city with a self-centred unspecialised economy with citizens providing for their own needs and making their own clothes, and an isolated city with minimal communication with the rest of the country.

Political stability came at the opportune moment when the new techniques of the industrial revolution were being introduced. The textile industry took root in the city and flourished despite the long time gap between the restricted transport afforded by turnpike roads and the late introduction of canal transport.

The role of the industrial entrepreneur has been traced from the wide-ranging Forster, whom misfortune, and perhaps over-ambition, brought untimely bankruptcy, to the industrial giants Ferguson, Dixon and McAlpin. These firms in turn were to meet with very different fortunes in later years. The greatest, Dixons, unable to adapt and in the radically changing circumstances following the American Civil War, met with disaster. Ferguson and McAlpin, although on a somewhat smaller scale, kept in the forefront of the ever changing technology, employed specialised staff, the chemist, artist and engraver and produced a highly sophisticated product that found a world market.

A revolution in transport accompanied the revolution in industry. At the end of the period under review, Carlisle had been opened up to the world through a succession of innovations of ever increasing importance, the turnpike road, the canal and finally the railway. If one event had to be selected to be the most significant symbol of Carlisle's integration into the national economy, a very strong case could be made out for the opening of the Carlisle Canal in 1823. It was an occasion of triumph and self congratulation, and the opportunity for the entire community to take part in a spectacular celebration. But the proprietors, through their failure to pluck up courage and build at the propitious moment, had lost their financial opportunity. They failed to anticipate that within a few years James Watt's steam engine would be adapted for locomotion by a new generation of engineers. The delay lost them their opportunity to get their capital back before their formidable competitor came on the scene.

The proprietors of the first railway from Carlisle, the Carlisle and Newcastle Railway, also misjudged the state of the art. Their proposal was indeed for a

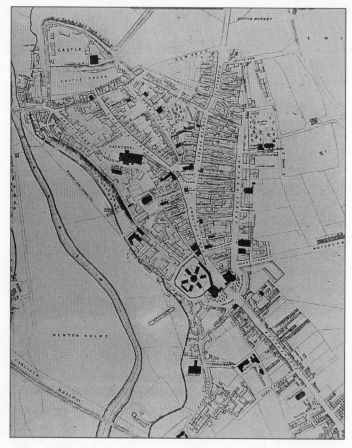

1842 – Studholme. Dense development along 'The Lanes' and along Corporation Dam. New model prison appears. Newcastle and Carlisle railway extended to canal basin. Warwick Road appears (named Henry Street and Botcherby Road).

railway, but the locomotive power was to be provided by horses. Fortunately the successful Manchester–Liverpool railway opened in time for the lesson to be learnt and the Carlisle–Newcastle line was opened using steam locomotives.

The opening of the canal, and the Carlisle–Newcastle railway, were not the culmination of the struggle of the Carlisle industrialists to gain a viable access to national and international markets. It turned out to be but one stage, and that fraught with hazard, before Carlisle was integrated into the national rail network at the end of the period under review. There was nothing inevitable in the triumph of Carlisle's industrialists. All the more therefore must they be praised for their courage.

But this brief review is a highly selective account of the development of Carlisle. Previous chapters have revealed a dichotomy between the local historians and compilers of directories, who wrote in an optimistic vein of progress to a better and more prosperous city, and the reports of Commissioners, and of certain newspaper reports, which recorded the poverty, oppression and appalling living conditions of large sections of the community, which cast doubts upon the whole concept of progress. In the early years of the nineteenth century, industrial enterprise could be correlated with social recession and degradation. The growth of material wealth and property led to a mushrooming of draconian laws to protect property; entrepreneurial dynamism in a competitive market was accompanied by a laissez faire attitude with left large groups of workers with a wage barely sufficient to support life; women and unprotected children of a tender age, were drawn into the factory system and worked horrendous hours, and this was justified on the grounds that it was necessary to retain overseas markets.

Urban poverty, and the absence of governmental control, led to overcrowding in slum property without the basic sanitary amenities necessary for a civilised life. With poverty and slums went disease and a high mortality rate, which reached a horrifying level for young children.

No one can condone the social evils that accompanied urban growth, and compounding these horrors of industrial life there was a general lowering of status and independence of the worker. Mr Mounsey, of Carlisle, gave evidence to the Walsham Committee on the deterioration in the position of the displaced agricultural worker who had been drawn into urban life.

Agricultural labourers, living in the country, with a comfortable cottage and garden, are certainly much better off than those living in Carlisle and earning little more than a common weaver without being able to get agricultural employment for their families, many of whom are brought up to weaving. There is little doubt that spinners and mechanics with families between 10 and 18 years of age earn more wages than labourers with families of the same age, but their means of expenditure make them worse off. Weavers living in the country and earning the same wages as those in the town are generally speaking, industrious and much better off than those in the town. The increased comforts of a country labourer with a more comfortable dwelling, better fed and clothed, his family always under his eye, and contented with his situation in life, tend to elevate him much above town labourers, and to withdraw him from public houses and the habits of intemperance to which they lead. His example too, together with the advantages of a village school, has a salutary influence on the habits and morals of his children and ensures to their parents in return a little pecuniary assistance in their old age.[1]

And yet looking back on the city's development in the first half of the nineteenth century one can see the accumulated effect of action taken in the political, social and educational fields that were to alleviate, if not to totally eradicate many of the social evils.

The mushrooming of laws prescribing the death penalty, or the lesser sentence of transportation, for comparatively minor offenses against property in the early years of the industrial revolution has been recorded with apprehension, but this was followed by Acts pruning away most of these horrendous penalties in the first half of the nineteenth century which provides evidence of real progress to a more humane society; and the substitution of graded prison sentences to fit the crime, made retribution in the Courts more certain by reducing the reluctance of the juries to convict. The Acts led to a dual benefit of making justice more certain and punishment more humane, but it also led to the need for new prisons for long term prisoners. The Act of 1839 for the better regulation of prisons enabled new types of prisons to be built to replace the 'Beggar's Opera' type of gaol. Within a few years of the Act being passed a new prison, built on the new theories, was built in Carlisle.

Important political legislation to increase the franchise was passed in the 1830s. The Reform Act of 1832 enacted that rights of voting in a Borough were to be enjoyed by every male person, the owner or tenant of a house of yearly value of not less than £10, whereas before parliamentary voting rights had been restricted to the 900 freemen of the city. Under the Numicipal Corporation Act of 1835, burgesses of the city who paid the rate for the relief of the poor became the electorate in the municipal election and thus breached the defence of the oligarchic City Corporation.[2] But the poor and under privileged were left as before with no voting rights at either parliamentary or municipal elections. They remained a discontented 'lower order' of society.

The legislation of the 1835 Act gave corporations powers to provide services and amenities, without having to apply for Special Acts of Parliament, but they were restricted in what they could do by the reluctance of the burgesses, the ratepayers, to foot the bill. It is a matter of regret that legislative measures did not make significant inroads on the appalling housing problems in the first half of the nineteenth century, but the social conscience, outraged by the findings of the Commissioners in 1845, was to be the driving force for action later in the century. One very significant step was, however, taken locally when the Carlisle Water Co. was formed in 1846 – a major pre-requisite for the provision of a pure drinking water supply and for a more civilised sewage disposal system.

The Parliamentary Acts for the regulation of labour in textile factories in the nineteenth century bring into stark relief the inhumanity of the early unregulated factory systems, but also record the series of small, if grudging, steps that over the first third of the century brought about a considerably shorter working day and made possible some form of education for the factory child.[3] The 1833 Act[4] which prohibited the employment of children under 9, restricted children under 13 to a 48 hour week, and young people of 13 to 18 years to a 69 hour week, also introduced an important innovation that stipulated that the younger children, those restricted to a 48 hour week, should receive 2 hours schooling on each week day. Mannix and Whellan noted that the Shaddongate School, opened in 1836, 'is chiefly supported by Messrs Peter

Dixon & Sons to whom great praise is due for their laudable exertion in facilitating the education of the offspring of the operative classes. The children pay 2 pence a week.' In 1847 there were 180 children of both sexes in the school.[5] But the pursuit of a Social theme has introduced this school prematurely for a chronological educational sequence.

The main educational facilities in Carlisle grew steadily from an exceedingly low base in the late eighteenth century and by 1861 no less than 5,006 children, almost equally divided between boys and girls, were classified as scholars in the census.[6] This spectacular increase, in the absence of Government funding, and with the Parish vestries unwilling to levy a rate to promote education, was due mainly to the intervention of the church. The educational facilities made available by the various churches, with their limited resources, were impressive and should be judged against the almost total lack of organised education in the previous century, rather than against modern educational standards. While the educational system was primarily concerned with improving the live of people and social cohesion a vital ingredients in the early 19th century was th provision of an incresing supply of competent people to service the administration and technical needs of a growing industrial society. A short digression on the growth of schools in Carlisle will record the magnitude of the achievement, but will also reveal the discontinuity in the growth, and the limitations of the education provided.

The Grammar School was founded in the sixteenth century to provide an elitist classical education,[7] but by the eighteenth century grammar schools were in decline in the country as a whole, and in Carlisle in particular. It is said that at one time late in the century the pupils at the Carlisle Grammar School numbered no more than 4 boys.[8] Early curriculums of Grammar Schools had been founded on classical Latin and Greek studies from the Elizabethan era with little account of subjects developed since that time and was largely irrelevant to the needs of a developing industrial society. It was only in the early 19th century that this curriculum was broadened. There was a revival in the early years in the nineteenth century when the school had 40–50 pupils[9] and by the mid-century the school was expanding and intrestingly these are records of boarders housed in masters houses, and it became necessary to move to the present handsome building in Swifts Lane in 1883.[10] With an elitist educational system no longer in favour, it has in recent years been reformed as Trinity School.

Systematic attempts to provide an elementary education can be traced back to the eighteenth century when charity schools and Sunday schools first made their appearance. Charity schools were established for the education of the poor and free instruction, along with free meals and clothing, provided a basic level of literacy, at least the ability to read, and sometimes to write and perform simple arithmetical sums. Surprisingly the first reference to a charity school in

Carlisle, was for the education, not of boys, but for the daughters of poor freemen. The school, which was in existence in 1790 provided clothing and taught the girls to read, knit and sew.[11] The chief source of elementary education at this time, however, were the Sunday schools which started to proliferate in England form c. 1780. The professed purpose of the Sunday school movement was to teach children to read the bible and to accept their position in Society, but they became much more than an instrument of social control and their educational value was enhanced by the teaching of writing and some arithmetic. The hours of instruction on a Sunday could amount to 4 to 6 hours[12] and severe demands were made upon the students, many of who had endured long hours in the factory during the week. The number of Sunday schools in Carlisle at the turn of the century is uncertain, but the Universal Directory of 1790 refers to Sunday schools in the plural and the Jollie Directory of 1811 refers to several Sunday schools. Himmelfarb opines that the average length of attendance at Sunday schools was 4 years and that some children supplemented their education with intermittent spells at a day school.[13] A form of education at the turn of the century, with a more explicit social content was the School of Industry in Carlisle where Jollie records 30 girls were taught sewing, writing and reading. In the early nineteenth century the Church and voluntary organisations accepted the daunting challenge to provide primary education, and introduced radically new concepts in the organisation of teaching, and in the design of school buildings. Two noted pioneers were Joseph Lancaster, a Quaker, who set up the British and Foreign Schools Society and Andrew Bell, a Church of England clergyman, who founded the National Society. Both Societies used the monitorial system in which a single teacher taught a small number of the older and more able children, who in turn each taught a group of children in the class. Inevitably the teaching was by rote.[14] The simultaneous teaching of many groups of children in one large classroom was a mass production form of tuition and it is tempting to draw an analogy with the contemporary cotton factory turning out its cheap and standardised product. The Lancastrian School opened in 1811 with a large room in Watergate with 170 children.[15] Subsequently, it was moved to Mary Street where two rooms were occupied, on average, by 100 boys and 70 girls.[16] The National School building, named the Central School, was built in 1812 on West Walls adjacent to Sally Port. Two 'spacious' rooms to house 220 boys and 180 girls were provided.[17] It has been estimated that the cost of educating a child was 7 shillings a year. The next school to be built, St Patrick's Day and Sunday school, was under Catholic Sponsorship, but children of all denominations were accepted. It opened in 1826 with 200 boys and girls.[18]

In 1829 there were in total 905 pupils at the elementary day schools and 1,360 pupils at the Sunday schools,[19] but in addition to the facilities provided by the large educational institutions there is ample evidence of a search for improvement for those who were prepared to pay. The Parson and White

Directory of 1829 lists many establishments, based upon modest sized private houses. There were 3 gentleman's boarding schools, each run by a clergyman, 2 ladies boarding schools and 22 additional day schools.[20] In 1843 there was the first mention of a state grant for education when 2 national schools were built, Trinity Schools in Caldewgate, and Christ Church School in Botchergate. The latter school received a parliamentary grant for a school house in Crown Street.[21] There was a welcome sign that some regard was now paid to the needs of children as play grounds were introduced for the first time. Mannix and Whellan inform us that in 1847 there were 4,000 children in regular attendance at the various Sunday schools 'for which Carlisle is pre-eminent.'[22]

There was one group of children who had hitherto been missed out of the educational process. These were the children of the 'ragged classes' who, ragged both literally and in self regard, shrank from attending the established schools. The 'Ragged schools Union' was established in 1844 under the presidency of Lord Ashley. The name 'ragged' was derogatory, even in the plain speaking nineteenth century some people were reluctant to use it, but Lord Ashley confessed that upon reflection he decided that it did have the great merit of reassuring those for whom the schools were intended and who might be put off by a more conventional sounding name.[23] It would seem that the Ragged schools in Shaddongate must have been nearly contemporary with the founding of the Union as their presence is noted in the 1858 Directory and Guide to Carlisle.

Fundamental changes were introduced for the provision of elementary education by the Education Act of 1870 which set out to supplement existing education, and ultimately to replace, voluntary schools with state schools. The system was controlled by School Boards elected by rate payers empowered to raise funds from the local rates. The School leaving age was eventually raised to 13.

The 1902 Education Act abolished school boards and transferred their powers to local education authorities, and in addition made provision for secondary and technical education.In the Grammar School extended facilities were made for admission to the school, and the Governing Body ???? to include representatives not only of the Abbey, but also of the city and County.

Townscape

In physical appearance Carlisle had changed vastly from Hutchinson's description of the city in the early eighteenth century when

Carlisle at the beginning of the present century exhibited no marks of modern convenience and elegance. The buildings mostly of wood, clay and lathe bespoke of the poverty and bad taste of the inhabitants.

In sharp contrast Mannix and Whellan recorded their general impressions of the city in 1847 the city which now contains many elegant houses and public edifices. English Street, Scotch Street and Castle Street diverging from the market place are spacious and contain many well stocked shops . . . The market place is lined with well stocked retail shops, and the city possesses several commodious and comfortable inns with 3 excellent hotels, and within a circuit of 10 miles round Carlisle are numerous beautiful castle and villas.[24]

There were indeed many shops in mid-century Carlisle, as Appendix No. 4 will confirm, and there were some fine new public buildings. Jefferson describes the Reading Rooms at the corner of English Street and Devonshire Street, completed in 1831, but later unfortunately replaced by a Bank.

. . . it is a very elegant modern structure, composed of white free stone and exhibiting a beautiful example of the Decorated style of Gothic architecture . . . the south west front consists of a gabled centre flanked by two wings with embattled parapets . . . the elevation in Devonshire Street is more extended; it contains in the centre a fine Oriel, all the lights of which have crocheted canopies, its buttresses are particularly light and elegant; and are crowned with enriched pinnacles.[25]

Atheneaum, Lowther Street, Classical building with Corinthian Pilasters. Home of Mechanics Institute (1840) now Trustee Savings Bank.

Subscription News Room and Library in English Street/Devonshire Street by
Thomas Rickman in Gothic style(1831). Now greatly altered and converted to
Cumberland Building Society.

Another fine building, the Cumberland Infirmary, erected on high ground
overlooking the Canal Basin still exists, although now as part of a much larger
complex. Jefferson wrote

> . . . it is an extensive and very handsome white free stone building erected
> by subscription; the foundation stone was laid 1st October 1830 . . . It is a
> tetrastyle, with a portico with four Grecian Doric Columns; and it is the
> only example of the ancient or classical architecture exhibited in the public
> buildings of Carlisle.[26]

But it was not long before another fine example of classical architecture appeared
in Carlisle. The Athenaeum, in Lowther Street opposite to Devonshire Street,
was built in 1840. Mannix and Whellan describe its 'Roman style' of architecture
with its fine facade punctuated with massive pilasters surmounted with Corinthian capitals.[27] This building is now occupied by a bank but the facade remains.

But it was not only the grand buildings that were transforming Carlisle in
the mid nineteenth century; there was a corresponding growth in the supply
of domestic houses. Whellan writing in 1860 gave evidence of new housing
developments.

> There are few towns in England that have made more rapid strides in social
> and material advancement than Carlisle. In a single decade the face of the
> town has been almost entirely changed . . . streets of houses, of massive

Citadel Station in Tudor style by William Tite with mullioned and transomed windows and Clock Tower (1847/8).

form, with all the conveniences that modern art can suggest . . . have sprung up as residences for the merchant and the manufacturer, and the tradesman. Streets of houses, too, have been erected for the working man, in lieu of dingy alleys, creaking garrets, and fever stricken yards. The clerk, the merchant, and even the labourer, has had his dwelling improved and now enjoys the freshness of the fields and the recreation derived from the cultivation of his little plot of garden ground.[28]

The most striking housing development occurred when the Denton Holme estate was split up and sold for housing development. The construction of the Nelson Bridge across the River Caldew in 1853, which connected Denton Holme directly with the heart of the city, greatly facilitated this development. This area, in which the industrial and residential uses of land are closely interwoven, catered for a working class population but as it came under the general supervision of the local Board of Health minimum building standard were enforced, and in 1859 back to back housing prohibited. The artisan classes were soon attracted from the lanes and courts of the old central core of the city.

The first Ordnance Survey Map c. 1860. shows the addition of Nelson Bridge and the back bone of streets in Denton Holme viz Denton Street, Charlotte Street, Millbourne Street, and Junction Street to link up with Dalston Road. This basic network was rapidly filled up with interconnecting streets in the following decades. The rapid growth of Denton Holme is made manifest in the population statistics. In 1841 there were 460 inhabitants. The corresponding figures for 1851 and 1861 were 780, and 2,800.[29]

With the improved housing stock went better services, a better water supply, and an improved, but still imperfect, sewerage system. But perhaps it was the improved gas supply which followed the building of a much larger gas works in Borough Mill Field (adjacent to the Viaduct), that made the greatest visual impression, with the transformation of the night scene in the city. Whellan wrote:

> Previous to that time the town was indifferently lighted by a private company carrying on business at the head of Brown's Row – on the ground now spanned by the railway arch at the south end of the station. To say nothing of the reduction that was made in the rates charged upon consumers of gas, the facilities offered by the corporation, when the old company broke up and the new works were built under their direction, the benefits to private consumers and to the town especially, were most important. Since then the town has been well lighted on the whole; shopkeepers can afford to keep flaming lights in their windows and nearly the whole of the cottage property that has since been built is provided with gas. The dim light of a halfpenny candle is superseded by a flame that illuminates the whole house, at a much cheaper rate.[30]

But there is more quantitative evidence of social and economic progress. A set of statistics proposed by Feinstein as a measure of the standard of living assert that the 'Real consumption her head' for the country as a whole, more than doubled from 1761 to 1861,[31] though admittedly the figures are averaged for the economy as a whole and do not show up the inequalities that reduced the hand loom weaver to near starvation. The contention of increased material wealth among the citizens as a whole is supported by an analysis of Carlisle trade directories from 1790 to 1858 which show an increasingly specialised society with an ever growing proportion of professional people, and of domestic manufacturers and shops, to supply the needs of the citizens.[32] A great transformation indeed from the self sufficient community of 1745.

The contention has been made in the introductory chapter that the mid eighteenth century marked the transition from a medieval society to an emergent industrial town. The contention is now made that the mid

J. D. Carr, a Quaker, 1806–1864. Founder of bakery and biscuit business, 1831. (*Carlisle Library*)

nineteenth century marks the transition from a vigorous, but dangerously narrow based, industrial society to one more diversified and more stable, and recognisably akin to the modern city. There are early signs of this transformation in the 1861 census, a census which classifies the inhabitants of the city according to their occupation. The census reveals that the cotton industry, which employed 4,225 people, of which 54% were female, was the main source of livelihood of the inhabitants but there were significant other sources of employment. On the industrial side the railways had created 574 jobs and no less that 860 people were employed in the building trades, indicative of the development and rebuilding that was going on in the city at this time. But there are other, and perhaps more far-reaching changes in the structure of society, which are revealed in the census. Firstly there is the growth of service industries which would eventually outgrow the industrial sector. Significantly there were 1,000 domestic servants in 1861 which were to increase 40% in the next 4 years.

Secondly the listing of 43 Post Office workers and 64 clerical workers provides an early indication of the beginning of a change in the structure of trade and industry to a more complex society where the clerical worker, those who administer and record, would stand comparison with the 'makers of goods'; in a later day terminology where the white collar worker would match the blue collar worker.

It was providential for Carlisle citizens that new sources of employment were opening up as the cotton industry was, in the 1860s, in decline, with the number of hand loom weavers rapidly dwindling and, in 1872, Dixon's, the greatest of the Carlisle cotton firms being declared bankrupt. Carlisle could not live by an emasculated cotton industry and service industries alone, but the railways gave employment in their own right, and by stimulating ancillary

Carr's, c.1834. Canal basin with sailing vessel in background. (*Tullie House*)

Carr's, pre-1900. No signs of tram-lines or overhead line supports. (*Carlisle Journal*)

J. D. CARR,

RESPECTFULLY informs his Friends and the Public, that he has commenced BUSINESS as a BAKER, and DEALER in MEAL and FLOUR, in CASTLE STREET, CARLISLE, nearly Opposite the CATHEDRAL; and hopes, by keeping Articles of the best Quality, with strict and persevering Attention, he will be entitled to a Share of the Public Support.
Carlisle, 6th Mo. 29th, 1831.

trades, but more than that they opened out markets for major Carlisle firms that were to come into increased prominence in the second half of the nineteenth century. It is outside the scope of this work to do more than summarise the early history of the major Carlisle non-textile firms that were to form the prologue to the next great stage of development in the Carlisle economy.[33]

Carr's of Carlisle was founded by Jonathan Dodgson Carr and developed rapidly in his life time. By the time of his death, in the latter half of the nineteenth century, the firm had 4 flour mills and a small fleet of coastal vessels to serve his bread bakeries and biscuit manufactory. The firm continued to expand and flourish under Theodore Carr, the eldest grandson of the founder.

Hudson Scott. Earlier mention has been made of Benjamin Scott who set up a small business in English Street in 1775. The business was developed by his nephew Hudson Scott who, in due course, was joined by his two sons Benjamin and William. A private company, formed under the name Hudson Scott and Sons, transferred the business of printing and box making to a new factory in

Ronald Carr, driving a steam car with a most distictive condenser. Of techincal interest because the steam car immediately proceeded the internal combustion engine. (*Tullie House*)

James Street *c.* 1870. The expansion which followed this move was to make them one of the major industries in Carlisle. In the next century the firm was merged with the Metal Box Co.

Cowans Sheldon were pioneers in designing and manufacturing steam travelling cranes. John Cowans and E. P. Sheldon, who had both served apprenticeships with Robert Stephenson, the great railway engineer, founded their firm at Woodbank in 1846 but moved to their site, between St Nicholas Street and London Road, in 1857.

On a smaller, but still significant scale, a number of Iron and Engineering trades played an important role in the city in the second half of the nineteenth century, particularly in Workshops connected with the railways. The L. N. W. Railway Co. built an engine works at St Nicholas and the Caledonian Co. built repair workshops at Elferby, and at a later date, then Midland railway built their workshops at Durran Hill. Other firms engaged in the iron and engineering trades were the Waterloo and the Victoria foundry companies and the long established firm of Porter, Hinde and Porter in Blackfriars Street. Another firm that expanded in the later part of the nineteenth century was William Carrick & Sons, who had started the manufacture of high grade felt hats in 1790 in Borough Street but moved to Norfolk Street when the former street was cleared to make way for the building of the Citadel Station.

The study has ended on an optimistic note, made more so perhaps, by the quotations from various nineteenth century 'Histories', with their bland outlook on the current state, and future outlook of the city. This is not to disparage the progress made to a more affluent, more pleasant and indeed more healthy city, but only to emphasise the enigmatic nature of 'progress'.

The concept of progress of the city, if it can be vindicated must rest partly on the efforts of a dynamic entrepreneurial class who exploited economic opportunities made possible by technical innovations; partly as the result of equally dynamic efforts of social investigators and reformers, and partly as the result of enlightened self interest of citizens who saw that social, and in particular health hazards, could not be restricted to one section of the citizens, but must eventually effect all. A wide overall review of the economic and social condition of the city and its inhabitants support the concept of

John Cowans, co-founder of Cowan's Sheldon, 1857. (*Tullie House*)

economic progress. It is indisputable that the industrial base of the city had been widened and that the citizens were not so vulnerable to catastrophic trade depression caused by dependence on a highly specialised economy linked to an outmoded technology. For social progress the evidence is ambivalent but betterment can be claimed in spite of the continuance of a heterogeneous, class divided society. It is inconceivable that Chadwick's metaphor of the unknown foreign country[34] could still be applied to urban slums after the uninhibited discloses of the reports of the 1830s and 1840s, and the remedial action that had been taken, albeit not so comprehensively as could be hoped, but Disraeli's 'two nation' metaphor, which appeared in the sub title of his novel Sybil (1845), is more difficult to refute, but 'the poor', in a nation divided between 'the rich and the poor', is a less emotive variant of Chadwick's 'foreign nation'. But in spite of this general impression of social progress some unpleasant facts of life can still be discovered when searching through historical documents. Thus the Power Report of 1874, referring to Carlisle stated

> Enteric fever is habitually present, to a greater or lesser extent, and was rather seriously prevalent during the first quarter of the present year.
>
> The more recent epidemic of fever has been typhus, probably at first imported, and spreading under circumstances of crowding and squalor, till it has attained the proportions of a severe epidemic.[35]

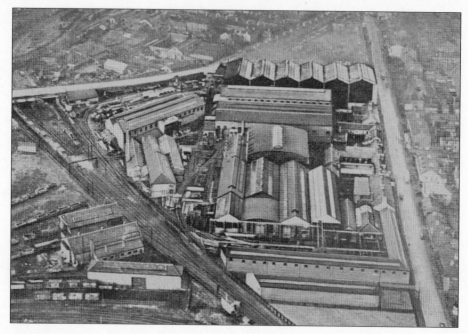

Cowans Sheldon, St Nicolas Works. (*County Library*)

Progress in the city in the period under review was not a gradual and steady ascent, but consisted of the summation of positive and negative factors in the wide fluctuations of the fortunes and misfortunes of individuals and, in particular, of different classes of society. Only from the vantage point of a later age will the historical perspective reveal an unmistakeable upward trend in human betterment.

NOTES

1. Sir John Walsham, *First Report on the State of the Dwellings of the Labouring Classes (No. 24) Cumberland, Durham, Northumberland and Westmorland*, Political Tracts p. 1173 (1840), p. 438.
2. See Appendix No. 8.
3. See Appendix No. 5.
4. 3 and 4 William IV c. 103 (1833) *Act to Regulate Labour of Children and Young Persons in the Mills and Factories of the UK*.
5. Mannix and Whellan, *Directory of Cumberland* (1847), p. 139.
6. 1861 census.
7. T. Bulmer in his *History and Directory of East Cumberland* (1884) writes:

    Present school founded by Henry VIII. In the foundation statutes of the Cathedral of Carlisle he directs the Dean and Chapter to appoint one learned in Greek and Latin, of good reputation and pious life, endowed with the faculty of teaching, who shall train in piety and furnish with sound learning any boys, whatsoever, reporting to our school for sake of learning grammar.

8. C. F. C. Padel, *Historical Sketch, Carlisle Grammar School Memorial Register* 1264–1924 (1924), p. 23.

9. Parson and White, *History, Directory and Gazetteer of Counties of Cumberland and Westmorland* (1829), p. 144.

10. Padel, op. cit., pp. 24, 29.

11. W. Hutchinson, *History and Antiquities of Carlisle* (1794), p. 659.

12. Gertrude Himmelfarb, *The Idea of Poverty* (1984), p. 373.

13. Ibid.

14. The British and the National schools were similar in conception but distinctive in layout. The pupils in the British School were seated in a block in the centre of the room, facing the master's platform. The wide aisles were occupied when the pupils vacated their desks to practice their lessons under the supervision of the monitors. The layout of the National School was reversed with the seated area along the side walls, and a hollow square in the middle for the pupils to assemble in their groups. In both systems the children would alternate between periods of sitting and standing which was intended to maintain the alertness of the children. The alternation of position between groups of students also permitted a compact layout and a frugal provision of benches and desks.

15. Parson and White, op. cit., p. 144.

16. Mannix and Whellan, op. cit., p. 138.

17. Parson and White, op. cit., pp. 144–5.

18. Ibid.

19. Ibid.

20. Parson and White, op. cit., p. 159.

21. Mannix and Whellan, op. cit., p. 139.

22. Ibid.

23. Himmelfarb, op. cit., p. 375.

24. Mannix and Whellan, op. cit., p. 149.

25. S. Jefferson, *History and Antiquities of Carlisle* (1838), pp. 289–91.

26. Ibid.

27. Mannix and Whellan, op. cit., p. 140.

28. W. Whellan, *History of Cumberland and Westmorland* (1850), p. 96.

29. Ibid.

30. Whellan, op. cit., p. 96.

31. Feinstein C. H., *Capital Accumulation in the Industrial Revolution* (Economic History of Britain, edited by R. Floyd & D. McCloskey).

32. See Appendix No. 4.

33. I rely on the *Cumberland News Historical Exhibition Catalogue* (1951) for some of the detail in this section.

34. Edwin Chadwick in his *Report on the Sanitary Condition of the Labouring Population of Great Britain* (1842) Commented that the wealthier classes were often unaware of the condition of the poor, he said:

The statements of the condition of considerable proportions of the labouring population of the towns into which the present inquiries have been carried have been received with surprise by persons of the wealthier classes living in the immediate vicinity, to whom the facts were as strange as if they related to foreigners, or the natives of an unknown country . . . We found that the inhabitants of the front houses in many of the main streets of those towns and the metropolis, had never entered the adjoining courts, or seen the interiors of any of the tenements, situated at the backs of their own houses, in which their own workpeople reside (p. 397).

35. W. H. Power, *Report to the Local Government Board on Recent Epidemic Prevalence of Fever in Carlisle, and on the Sanitary State of the City* (1874) (Cumbria Record Office).

Postscript

Carlisle's industrial structure was again transformed in the twentieth century, particularly after the Second World War. In spite of two world wars and the economic depression of the 1930s citizens became more prosperous. There was a relative growth in the service sector in relation to the manufacturing industry as the demand for basic material goods were gradually met and the demand for services, such as for administration, for a more complex society, and for citizens requirements in health, education, transport, civic amenities and tourism. In 1991 while 64% of the workforce were employed in the service industries, a mere 22% were employed in manufacturing[1] – a figure below the proportion employed in textiles alone in 1861 (Appendix 7), bearing in mind that the textile industry was already in decline in that year particularly among the hand loom weavers. Comparison of census figures for 1861 and 1901 (Appendix 7) reveal a great increase in the number of people employed in transport, and food, drink and clothing retailing. Napoleon's gibe about England being a nation of shopkeepers greatly understated the numbers employed in retailing at the end of the nineteenth century.

The 1861 and 1901 census returns record a relative decline in the textile industry in Carlisle which continued in the next century. The occupational structure was also changing, female domestic service became a very prominent feature of England life until World War II, after which secretarial and administrative work became important for female employment.

Sadly the twentieth century witnessed the demise of many of the giant firms of the nineteenth century, but in the broader picture the change in structure has been beneficial, with the majority of firms with a work force of less than 500 in place of nineteenth century firms of over 1,000 workers only matched now by small number of firms such as United Biscuits (Carrs), Cavaghan and Gray and Pirelli. Industry is no longer centralised in the urban area along the River Caldew but in industrial estates outside the city centre. The largest estate at Kingstown employs 2,000 workers while smaller estates have been developed at Rosehill, Willow Holme, Burgh Road, Durranhill and Newtown Road.

Carlisle is well served with its diversified industries and its expanding services and administrative sectors. In 1993 Carlisle was in the top flight of business successes. In a 1994 survey from Dun and Bradstreet International Carlisle was top of a league table of corporate successes with 83.9% of business in the city making a profit, and with an unemployment rate of 7.7% against a national average of 11.2% in Great Britain and 13.4% in the north.

The following gazetteer lists the larger Carlisle firms with a broad indication of the size of their workforce.[2]

Twentieth-Century Carlisle Industry Gazetteer

Fergusons, Holme Head

In the early twentieth century large extensions were made to the spinning and weaving machinery, the printing, dyeing and bleach works and the finishing plant, so that by the centenary date of 1924 the firm with a work force of 1,400 was a major cotton manufacturer of worldwide repute producing an extensive assortment of coloured cotton fabrics and combinations of cotton and real and artificial silk. The firm gained many national and international awards, perhaps the most outstanding being the award granted by the United States Centennial Commission for the International Exhibition at Philadelphia in 1876 with a citation 'Fineness of texture, superior colours, superb dyeing, with a finish of remarkable excellence. The harmony and blending of colours are exceedingly fine.'

In the post World War II years however the firm was in decline and in 1966 it was taken over by Viyella. The print works were demolished and only part of the weaving section used. Now the firm is part of the Carrington Novare Group with a modest work force in the 50–100 range.

Stead McAlpin

Screen printing was introduced in the 1930s and a new shop was built for that purpose. Post World War II, the first became part of the John Lewis Partnership although still trading under its own name as a textile printer. It employs a work force in the 250–500 range.

Dixon's Shaddon Mill

It has already been recorded that the Dixon firm was declared bankrupt in 1872 and after resurrected as a joint stock company it finally cased to trade in 1883.

In 1888 it was reoccupied by Robert Todd and converted to woollen spinning and as such survived for nearly 100 years, William Linton, who came to Carlisle in 1912 occupied the weaving sheds and today provides high class fabrics for ladies fashion houses throughout the world.

The Dixon Langthwaite Mill was taken over by the Otterburn Tweed Co. in 1883 but closed in 1977. The factory is now occupied by separate business units.

The 'deferential society' – the hiring of 1904. The lady seals the contract with 1s. (*Templeton Collection*)

The Green Market, *c.* 1890. (*County Library*)

Cowans Sheldon

On moving to their new site between St Nicholas Street and London Road in 1869 the partners built up a major general engineering firm principally manufacturing articles connected with railways and docks. The site, adjacent to the Southbound railway was ideally suited for a major customer. The great speciality of the firm was the building of cranes, fixed or mobile, for travelling on land and sea, first powered by steam, then hydraulic or pneumatic, and finally by electric power. In 1925 they built a colossal floating crane for Japan with a working capacity of 350 tons, and a height from the water to the tip of the jib of 245ft.

In the post war years the firm was taken over successively by Clarke Chapman,

N. E. Industries and Cowan Boyd. Gradually the work was taken away from Carlisle eventually resulting in the closure of the site and its subsequent redevelopment as a retail park. The work of the firms' design offices however are still retained in the city operating from the former Carlisle Corporation Electricity Building on James Street now converted to the City Council's Enterprise Centre.

Carrs (United Biscuits)

The firm continued to flourish in the late nineteenth century and twentieth century. In 1928 the workforce reached 3,000 people, there was a slight decrease to 2,700 workers in 1954 of whom half were women. The firm in the post war days of big mergers was taken over by Cavenham Foods in 1964 and then became part of the McVities and United Biscuit Group. The firm now employs between 1,200 and 2,000 (peak season).

Carrs (Silloth)

In 1887 Carrs erected a large flour mill at the dock side at Silloth. It was later incorporated as a limited company with a workforce range of 50–100.

Hudson Scott

Opened a new factory in James Street in 1868. In 1898 a limited company was formed. In 1906 the workforce had expanded to 1,200 of whom one half were girls. In 1922 they amalgamated with similar firms to form the Metal Box Company. The firm was directed by F. N. Hepworth for nearly forty years before his retirement in 1945.

The firm is now part of Carnaud Metal Box with a workforce in the range of 250–500.

Morton Sundour

Established when James Morton came to Carlisle in 1900 and helped by his father set up a factory at Denton, formerly occupied by Donalds which was powered by water from a tail race from Holme Head known as the Little Caldew. The firm which became an acknowledged leader in high quality fabrics was taken over by Courtaulds in 1965 and shut down to be replaced by Gleneden Textiles, a subsidiary of Courtaulds, who produce fabrics for the automobile industry.

Bucks

R. Buck in 1882 set up Atlas Works, Nelson Street to manufacture shirts, pyjamas and scarves. At one time the firm employed 500 people. In 1984 the factory was taken over by Bonsoir but closed in 1986.

Carlisle Gas Works, Bousteads Grassing, 1928. (*Carlisle Journal*)

Willow Holme
Power Station.
(*Carlisle Journal*)

R. R. Buck and
Sons, Atlas
Works. (*Carlisle
Journal*)

Carr's Flour Mill, Silloth (1887, enlarged 1904). (*Carlisle Journal*)

Silloth. Solway and pier at harbour entrance. The pier was damaged and destroyed in the mid-twentieth century.

Carricks South Vale Hat Works

Established 1790 for manufacture of high grade felt hats. In the late nineteenth century the firm moved to Norfolk Street when the railway was built over their original site in Borough Street. The firms survived into the post world war years but has now gone.

John Laing

This major national and international firm started as builders in Carlisle in 1874 by John Laing (1842–1924). The firm continued to prosper under his son, Sir John Laing (1879–1979), and was responsible for a very high proportion of major projects in the Carlisle area, including a major role in the construction of a 300 acre township for munition workers (1914–18) at Gretna and the inter-war Carlisle housing estates. In 1926 the head office was moved to London while the N. W. branch office remained in Dalston Road, Carlisle. Post World War II, the firms were responsible for major works such as the Windscale Nuclear Energy Station and the M1 Motorway between London and Birmingham.

Sir John (1879–1979) and Lady Laing after the consecration of Coventry Cathedral 1962. (*County Library*)

Issac Teasdale

In 1872 took over the firm of Thomas Halstead, makers of boiled sweets, jams, etc. Post War the firm went into liquidation and the factory taken over by the Penguin Confectionery Company.

Pratchett Brothers

Denton Ironworks established 1859, manufactured plant and equipment to customers designs and specifications. Became part of L. A. Mitchell, suppliers of equipment to chemical industry in the 1960s. Now part of A. P. V. Mitchell Driver Ltd., manufacturer of industrial dryers, etc.

William Coulthard

Manufacturer of die-casting plant. Founded 1880 in Castle Street. Moved to Lonsdale Street in 1878 and Crown Works in 1925. In 1949 Moved to Durranhill Trading Estate.

Allied Signal Ltd (Kangol)

Seat belts and safety equipment.

Cabaghan and Gray Ltd

Founded Harraby 1912. Fresh food manufacturer and supplier to Marks and Spencer and to European market, employ 1000+.

Nestle U. Ltd

Set up for milk processing at Dalston in the post war years.

Pirelli

Dalston Road. Car tyres, etc. Employs over 500 people.

Electrolux Klippan Ltd

Byron St. Caldewgate, manufacturer of child safety products and seat belts.

James Bendall and Sons

Albion Works, London Road. Sheet Metal fabricators and motorbody repairs.

Eden Construction

Durranhill, Carlisle CA1 3NB.

Electricity Generating Station James St.

Opened in 1899. A vastly increased demand by 1926 necessitated a new power station at Willow Holme. Ample cooling water from R. Eden obvited the need for cooling towers.

Gas Works Bowstead's Grassing

Increase in demand for gas led to a new works to be built.

This review of Carlisle over this last two and a half centuries has highlighted some striking scientific and technological discoveries that have transformed industry and the way we live. One can mention in ascending order of innovation and unpredictability the mechanisation of the cotton industry, steam power and the railway, and electric power that has transformed industry and the domestic economy. But the most striking innovation of all, that could not be envisaged even by the scientific fiction writer, at the beginning of the 20th century, is nuclear power, and the consequent establishment of the nuclear industry in West Cumberland within the last 50 years. British Nuclear Fuels is a great industry working at the frontiers of science and technology is now firmly established at Sellafield, with a workforce of 8,600 and an additional force of 1,500 sub-contractors, it has transformed West Cumbria economy. Seventy-five per cent of its workforce live in the Copeland region of Cumbria, the remainder in Allendale but with a sizable contingent from Carlisle. While

Hudson Scott's Works. (*Carlisle Journal, 1928*)

Carlisle is on the periphery of this industry it will inevitably prove to be a powerful stimulus to the economy in the future as in the past and provide exciting career opportunities and jobs for Carlisle young people. The future is hidden but Carlisle must be ready to stake a claim in a wider economy, geographically extended, increasingly sophisticated. They must meet the challenges of the future as they have successfully done in the past.

NOTES

1. Source 1991 OPCS Census 10% Sample.
2. Sources Carlisle City Council, Carlisle Industry and Commerce Directory (first edition) 1994.

Appendix 1

The Technology of the Cotton Industry

Weaving

1733 John Kay's Flying Shuttle. Shuttles mounted on Wheels, struck by a hammer to drive it through the warp. Weaver enabled to make a width of cloth that previously required work of two men. Mechanical difficulties delayed its widespread use until the 1750s and 1760s.

Spinning

c. 1750. Spinner used a single hand-wheel which was not capable of producing cotton warp in large quantities. (Linen normally used for warp). Spinning was the bottleneck in the industry.

1767 Hargreaves Spinning Jenny (patented 1770). Operated by one person. Small enough to fit into existing frame-work of domestic industry and did not require external source of power. Initially four spindles to each set of gearing, but larger frames, with multiples of four spindles, eventually reached a total of eighty spindles. Spinners now able to keep pace with the weaver and made possible a balanced family economy. But yarn was soft and only suitable for weft.

Spinning by jenny reached its peak in the 1780s. Spinning performed in a room of a cottage or in workshops from converted cottages.

1769 Arkwright's Water-Frame. Made of wood with brass gearing. Driven by water-power (hence the name) to give rise to the factory system. A rather course, but strong, cotton twist produced suitable for warps. A new product now possible, a cotton cloth that was not a mixture of linen warp and cotton weft.

1785 Cancellation of Arkwright's patents permitted widespread use of water-frames with as many as forty-eight spindles, the size increasing to possibly one hundred by year 1800.

1785 Jenny and water-frame now dominant and produced a variety of fustians, velvets and calicoes. The cheap calicoes were the first product of the industrial revolution. There was an eightfold increase in raw cotton imports between 1780 and 1800.

1775 Arkwright Carding Engine which lined up fibres of raw cotton into slivers, patented.

1800 Arkwright Roving Frame passed the slivers through rollers to draw them out, and the flyers put in the twist before feeding to the spinning machines. The carding engine and roving frame required power and operated side by side with the water-frame in the factory. An integrated factory system.

1779 Crompton's Mule The mule (the mating of a water-frame with a jenny) unlike the water-frame or the jenny, could produce the fine yarns (high counts) required for the top and expensive end of the Market. The mule was introduced slowly and made its impact in the late 1780s, but remained part of the domestic system until the 1790s. The carriage, containing up to 150 spindles, required great manual strength to operate. The application of water power to improved and enlarged machines made find spinning practicable on a large scale with greatly reduced prices. Watt's rotative double acting condensing engine of 1782 made steam power attractive and permitted the siting of large spinning factories in towns.

1800 Throstle frame (named from singing sound it made). Made of iron-framing and cast-iron gears. A simplification of the water-frame with the flyers, bobbins and rollers remaining the same, but the strong gearing and steam power permitted a great increase in size with only one or two sets of gearing.

c. 1790–1800 The abundant supply of yarn produced changed the character of the industry. Spinners now concentrated in factories and weavers, often part-time workers from rural areas, could settle in towns and devote all their time to weaving.

1800 The Semi Power Mule Up to 400 spindles per mule. The operator could set up one machine by hand while the other machine was drawing out and spinning, but the winding on sequence was not satisfactory.

1835 Roberts' Self Acting Mule A fully automatic machine, with a length of 120ft. and 1,200 spindles. The quadrant mechanism adjusted the speed of rotation of the spindles as the cop was built up.

Weaving

1785 Cartwright's power loom – initially primitive and did not make its impact until next century.

1780s and 1790s Increased output largely due to better organisation. Master Weavers employed festers (foremen) to control a large body of smaller weavers spread over a wide geographical area. Soon Master Weavers started moving their workers into weaving sheds.

c. 1820 Power looms first water driven then by steam. Power looms increased twenty-fold between 1813 and 1825 and a hundred-fold between 1813 and 1850. Cotton spinners tended to attach weaving sheds to their mills.

Bleaching

The first process of printing industry was to get a white cloth. The traditional method was to boil the fabric in a solution of ashes, then in sour milk, and to expose it to the weather in a 'Print Field' (the crofting process).

1756 Francis Holme in his 'Art of Bleaching' suggested use of sulphuric acid to replace sour milk which considerably speeded up the process.

1787 Bleaching by chlorine introduced from France.

1798 Charles Tennant produced a *bleaching powder* by passing chlorine gas over slaked lime. From the early 1800s the bleaching process was largely carried out indoors, superseding the crofting process. This released large areas of land formerly required for bleaching.

Printing

Late Eighteenth-Century Wooden-hand Blocks used to impress patterns on cloth. Then flat copper plates were substituted for wooden blocks.

1783 Thomas Bell introduced engraved cylinders, power driven.

The era of large scale production in calico printing practically coincided with developments in carding and spinning, but wood block techniques continued for the small scale luxury trade.

Appendix 2

1. Two Printfields appear on 1805 map. Donald (Willowholme) and Lamb (Damside).
2. Forster from 1801 to 1817. McAlpin took over mill in 1838.
3. Wood Bank on River Petteril, 2 miles south of Carlisle.
4. At Langthwaite Mill Warwick Bridge, Leased in 1790 to John, Richard and George Ferguson. By 1792 the factory was working with 443 spindles.
5. Shown on 1821 and/or 1842 maps.

Cotton Manufacturers 1794–1847

Parson & White Directory (1829) pp. 159–67		Mannix & Whellan (1847) pp. 145–7
Calico printers		
		Cummersdale[7]
Harrington, Wilde, Robley	Wood Bank	
W. Losh	Denton Holme[2]	
Bleaching		
Clarke, Robson	Sebergham Bridge[3]	'Several bleacheries'
Sanderson	Dalston	
Spinning		
11 Mills, collectively 80,000 spindles[8]		Collectively 122,000 spindles[9]
Cowen, Jacob	Watergate	4 mills at Carlisle including
Peter Dixon	Fisher Street	Dixon's (Shaddon Mills)[6]
Slater, New Mill	Watergate[5]	
Rothwell	Mains[5]	1 mill at Cummersdale
Carrick, Johnston, Blenkinson	Dalston	2 large mills at Dalston
R. & G. Cowen	Dalston	
J. Powsal	Dalston	
T. Sheffield	Dalston	
Gingham and Check Manufacturers		
Peter Dixon	Fisher Street[4]	'8 Gingham and Check
Ferguson, J. R. & J.	English Street[4]	Manufacturers'[9][10]
John Ferguson	Backhouse Walk[4][5]	
Robert Ferguson	Fisher Street	
Francis Stodhart	Finkle Street	
Robert Gale	Watergate	
Thos. Hunton	Lowther Street	
J. & D. Hewson	Drovers Lane	
Robert Hewson	Abbey Street	
Roper, Tweddle		
(Power Loom Weavers)	Long Island	

1. Term 'Printfields' had disappeared from the Jollie 1811 map. Presumably, new bleaching processes had superseded crofting process.
2. On the 'New Mill Race' Denton Holme.
3. Sobergham on River Caldew 6 miles south of Carlisle.
4. All considerable businesses with offices in Manchester.
5. Shown on 1821 and/or 1842 maps.
6. 'Peter Dixon & Sons, alone gave employment in the various departments of their cotton works to about 8000 hands' – Mannix & Whellan.
7. Presumably McAlpin (1835).
8. The eleven mills 'put in motion by means of 5 water-wheels and 6 steam engines

of an aggregate amount of power equal to the strength of 160 horses' – Parson & White.

9. 'The aggregate amount of power (for all cotton works) is equal to the strength of 510 horses; of this about 40 h. p. is by water' – Mannix & Whellan.

10. Presumably includes Joseph Ferguson Holme Head.

Appendix 3

Langthwaite Cotton Mill
Inventory of equipment December 1808

Garret	Two mules with 352 spindles each. These would be well suited for the production of the finer yarns (high counts).
High room	Two mules of 180 spindles each. Mawson suggests they may have been used for linen and wool.
Mid room	Four twist frames of 60 spindles each and 6 twist frames of 72 spindles each, together with 2 'water throstles'. Manders suggested that the 'water throstle' would be a water-powered version of the steam powered throstle. The twist frames and the 'water throstles' would have been suited for the production of twist (warp) yarn and the coarse threads for the lower (count) end of the market. The throstle frames and the mules would be complementary and taken together would cover a wide range of market needs.
Low room	Carding and roving machines.
Warping room	The warping mill could have prepared the warp beams for the weavers' looms.
Fancy dyehouse	Twenty jennies of 90 spindles each (in 'medium order'). These machines could have produced weft for the lower end of the market. Possibly because of their location and condition they may not have been operational.

Messrs Dixon & Sons were in the forefront of technological progress and correspondence with the Manchester firm of Sharp Roberts & Company refers to the purchase of a 'Danforth Throstle' in 1831. Manders suggests that this could be the Danforth Cap frame (patented in America in 1821 in his own name, and in England in 1829 in the name of Hutchinson) which became known as the Danforth Throstle Frame.

Information on the Langthwaite Mill and its equipment has been obtained from Langthwaite Cotton Mill by D. J. W. Mawson (Transactions of the Cumberland

& Westmorland Antiquarian & Archaeological Society. vol. LXXVI New Series 1976).

I am indebted to Mr R. G. Manders of the North Western Museum of Science and Industry Manchester for advice on the interpretation of the Inventory of Equipment, and on the Danforth Machine.

Appendix 4

Professions, traders and domestic manufacturers in Carlisle

	1790[1]	1811[2]	1847[3]	1858[4]
Population	8,000	11,500	28,000	36,000
Professions				
Physician	4	8	5	20
Chemist and druggist	2	3	16	16
Dentist	–	–	2	7
Architect and surveyor	–	3	3	10
Attorney and solicitor	19	14	22	21
Accountant	–	–	–	5
Auctioneer	–	1	5	5
Insurance agent	–	6	27	45
Traders				
Baker and flour distributor	1	9	25	6
Confectioner	3	6	18	14
Butcher	7	38	38	47
Fishmonger	–	–	6	10
Grocer and tea dealer	37	62	66	131
General dealer	–	–	75	33
Dressmaker and milliner	8	16	38	36
Draper	11	20	23	37
Clothier	–	–	14	14
Tailor	9	12	17	17
Domestic manufacturers and retailers				
Boots, shoes, clogs	12	30	74	40
Clocks and watches	2	5	9	11
Building Trades				
Bricklayer and stonemason	1	3	6	9
Slater	–	3	5	2
Joiner and Cabinet-maker	3	16	13	12
Painter, Glazier, Paperhanger	–	7	–	12

Hotels and Catering				
Inns, Taverns and Beerhouses	117	103	137	154
Eating Houses	–	–	–	10
Literary and Cultural				
News–agent	–	–	1	3
Reading rooms	–	–	5	9
Stationer and bookseller	3	2	9	12

The sources for the statistics are:
  1. Universal British Directory 1790
  2. Jollie's Directory 1811
  3. History, Gazetteer & Directory of Cumberland. Mannix & Whellan 1847
  4. Directory and Trade Directory. Published by Scott, Hudson 1858.

The 1790 and 1811 entries are for individuals, but two entries for one address are listed as one business.

The 1847 and 1858 entries refer to business.

While the trend of the figures are unmistakeable, their preciseness must be treated with caution because of possible differences of classification in the various Directories.

The Carlisle directories give evidence of the increasing complexity of the Carlisle economy. An increasing number of professional people to service society, of domestic manufacturers and shops to supply the needs of the citizens, and an increasingly specialised society contrasting with the largely self-sufficient families of 1745.

Carlisle throughout the period under review was very much a city of small shopkeepers and of domestic manufacturers not yet supplanted by the large scale manufacturers. People were becoming more literate with an increasing number of bookshops and reading rooms and with two weekly newspapers, the *Carlisle Journal* (Whig) founded in November 1798 and the Carlisle Patriot (Tory) founded in January 1815, the latter paper was renamed the Cumberland News in 1910.

Appendix 5

Parliamentary Legislation
to restrict the use of child labour in factories

The first Government legislation for the protection of children in cotton mills dates back to 1802.[1] It was to protect 'apprentices', often orphans or pauper children, drafted from large towns to mills in remote country areas where water power was available. The Act of 1802 limited apprentices to a 12-hour day, exclusive of meal times, between 6 a.m. and 9 p.m. and education for the apprentices was to be provided in some part of the building. The problem was given an extra dimension with the introduction of steam power. Cotton mills could now be built in urban areas where an abundant supply of labour was available and employers could employ local children. The Act of 1802 did not apply to these 'free' children.

Sir Robert Peel's committee was set up in 1816 to examine the expediency of a Bill to apply the provisions of the 1802 Act to all children who worked in factories. Speaking of a visit to his own factories Peel said:

> I was struck with the uniform appearances of bad health, and, in many cases, stunted growth, of the children. The hours of labour were regulated by the interests of the overseer, whose renumberation was regulated by the quantity of work done.

Peel expressed dissatisfaction with the conduct of his own overseers.

> If the limitation of 12 hours laid down in this Act had contented the overseers, I am persuaded that the health of the children would have been protected, but they frequently worked them 14 to 15 hours.[2]

The Act of 1819 followed. The employment of children under 9 years of age was prohibited and young persons under 16 were restricted to 12 hours a day.[3] In 1833, in the newly reformed Parliament, Lord Ashley (later to become Lord Shaftesbury the renowned philanthropist) presented his Ten-hour Bill which restricted young people, under the age of 18 years, to a working day of ten hours, but this met with a hostile reception. Opponents of the bill argued that British manufacturers would be unable to meet foreign competition. 'Machinery for the cotton industry was now being produced in France, and other places and spinning and the cotton manufactory was rapidly on the increase on the

Continent and the United States of America.' They argued that if the costs of the home industry were increased the cotton trade of this country might never recover.[4,5] The bill was defeated but a compromise government bill, proposed by Lord Althorp, the Chancellor of the Exchequer, was accepted by the House. The Act of 1833 prohibited the employment of children under 9. Children under 13 were restricted to 48 hours a week while young people between 3 and 18 were limited to 69 hours a week.[6] Unlike the earlier legislation the 1833 Act was given some teeth with the appointment of four inspectors to enforce the Act.

Something had been gained for the child under 13, but beyond that age the child entered the harsh world of the adult. There was, however, a gleam in the darkness. The Act decreed that the younger children, those restricted to a 8 hour day, should attend school. The child was required to produce a certificate each Monday morning confirming that he had attended school for two hours a day the previous week.

NOTES

1. Geo. III. C. 73 (1801–2). An Act for the Preservation of the Health and Morals of Apprentices and others employed in Cotton and other Mills, and Cotton and other Factories.
2. John Fielden The Curse of the Factory System (1836) pp. 9–10. Fielden was a large factory owner but also a reforming MP.
3. 59 Geo. III C. 66 (1819): 'To make further provisions for the Regulation of Cotton Mills and Factories, and for the better preservation of the health of Young Persons therein.'
4. Parliamentary Debates (1833) Hansard. Cols. 899–914.
5. Cotton consumption in Europe and America 1834.
   1,500,000 bales consumed annually averaging 300lbs each, of which
   940,000 bales consumed in Great Britain (i.e. nearly $\frac{2}{3}$
   280,000 bales consumed in France (i.e. nearly $\frac{1}{5}$
   216,000 bales consumed in America (i.e. nearly $\frac{1}{7}$
   64,000 bales consumed in other parts (i.e. $\frac{1}{24}$
   quoted from John Fielden. The Curse of the Factory System (1836) p. 57
6. 3 and 4 William IV C. 103 (1833) 'Act to regulate Labour of Children and Young Persons in the Mills and Factories of the UK.'

Appendix 6

The Dukery of Carlisle

James Losh in his 1826 diary referred to 4 or 5 houses in Carlisle belonging to the nouveaux riches.[1] Some of these were the industrialists prospering in the early nineteenth century who built up the resources to build stately villas outside the city to join the gentry.

Peter Dixon Junior picturesque house at Holme Eden designed by John Dobson, was built in 1837.

John Dixon, Peter's brother, MP twice Mayor and in 1838 High Sheriff, remodelled Knells in Grecian style in 1838.

Robert Ferguson bought Hawkes Lodge in 1807 and added the garden range, with flanking porches, in the classical idiom.

George Head, the founder of the first purpose-built bank in the city, rebuilt Rickerby House *c.* 1820 in Grecian style, later to become Eden School. The Lodge, fronting on to Linstock Road, is built in Doric temple style with an evocative inscription 'Study Quiet'.

Roberts Mounsey, Solicitor and calico printer built Castletown House, near Rockliffe, in Greek revival style *c.* 1811.

NOTE

1. *Country Life*, 11.8.89 and 7.9.89. Angus Taylor.

Appendix 7

1861 CENSUS						
Male Workers	10,826	% of total	Female Workers		7,936	% of total
Transport			Domestic Service		1,000	12.6
Road	161	1.5				
Railway	574	5.3				
Metal Workers	743	6.8				
Building	860	8.0				
Textiles	1,973	18.2	Textiles		2,252	28.4
Dress and Footware	620	5.7	Dress and Footware		746	9.4
Food, Drink, Tobacco, Lodgings	799	7.4	Food, Drink, Tobacco, Lodgings		382	4.8
Teachers	51	0.5	Teachers		74	0.8
Agriculture	563	5.2				
Scholars	2,468	22.8	Scholars		2,532	32.0
Clerks	64	0.6				
Others	1,950	18.0	Others		950	12.0
		100.0				100.0

1901 CENSUS						
Male Workers (10 yrs and over)	No.	% of total	Female Workers (10 yrs and over)		No.	% of total
Total occupied	13,579		Total occupied		6,486	
Transport	2,974	22.0	Domestic Servants		1,407	21.6
Engineering, Metal working	1,274	9.3	Laundry		147	2.3
Building and Construction	1,587	11.7	Teachers		257	4.0
Textiles	311	2.2	Textiles		1,097	16.9
Dress	721	5.3	Dress		924	14.2
Food, Drink, Tobacco, Lodging	1,470	10.0	Food, Drink, Tobacco, Lodging		1,085	16.7
Clerks	315	2.3				
Agriculture	207	1.5				
Others	4,720	35.7	Others		1,569	24.2
		100.0				100.0

Appendix 8

Parliamentary and Municipal Representation in Carlisle

The rights of local self government in Carlisle were founded on a series of royal charters granted to the city. The first charter was awarded by Henry II, but that and subsequent charters, granted by successive monarchs, were lost or destroyed before the union of England and Scotland. The governing charter of the city, prior to the Municipal Reform Act of 1835, was that granted by Charles I in 1637.[1]

The charter of Charles I enacted:

> . . . that in all time coming the mayor and citizens shall be one body corporate and politic, by the name of mayor, aldermen, bailiffs and citizens of the citizens of the city of Carlisle . . . That one of the aldermen shall be mayor: That there shall be besides the mayor eleven other aldermen, two bailiffs and two coroners: That there shall be within the said city 24 other men who shall be capital citizens, to be of the common council and assistance to the mayor, aldermen and bailiffs.

The form of government described in the charter was that of a self-perpetuating oligarchy. Thus

> The mayor, aldermen, bailiffs, and 24 capital citizens or the major part of them, would assemble in the Guildhall on the Monday next after Michaelmass day and would have power to chuse annually one of the aldermen to be mayor . . . who shall continue in office until another be chosen and sworn. In like manner two bailiffs and two coroners annually shall be chosen and sworn. On the death of an alderman, the mayor and surviving aldermen, in Guildhall assembled, shall chuse another who shall be sworn by the mayor, and to continue for life.
>
> Capital citizen dying, or for just cause removed, the mayor and aldermen shall chuse and swear another, who shall continue for life, unless by the mayor and aldermen for just cause removed.

The Corporation were given the power to make by-laws, and to enforce them by penalties corporal or pecuniary. The mayor, recorder and two senior aldermen, ex-officio, Justices of the Peace.[2] J.P.s were important figures in eighteenth-century England and had responsibilities for law and order, and administrative duties.

An important personage in the city was the freeman, or free burgess. He was a member of one of the eight guilds of Merchants, Butchers, Smiths, Tailors, Tanners, Weavers, Skinners and Shoemakers.

> No person can enjoy the privileges of a free burgess of Carlisle, unless he belongs to one of these guilds, to which none are admitted but the sons or apprentices of freemen . . . On a dispute in the House of Commons in 1711, it was declared that the sons of burgesses, born after their freedom, and persons serving seven years apprenticeship within the city have a right to be made free.[3]

But not all of the guilds were of equal status. Creighton writes

> Government of Carlisle originally in hands of Merchant Guild, but the rise of the Trade Guilds had compelled it to relax its autocracy and give some of them at least a control over its proceedings. For municipal affairs the Merchant Guild remained the governing body, but for all important matters it needed the consent of the Trade Guilds.[4]

But the freemen, as such, had lost some of their power. Parson and White writing in 1829 state

> The freemen to not now enjoy any peculiar immunities except the freedom from toll in the city, and the privilege of sending two representatives to Parliament.[5]

This was an important right in that the freemen of the city formed the electorate for parliamentary elections. And it was a sizeable electorate amounting to 'upward of 900'[6] in 1829 when the population was approximately 18,000. Carlisle's privilege of sending two representatives to parliament was of long standing and had been enjoyed since the reign of Edward I.[7] The elections in Carlisle were often conducted with great spirit and accompanied by riots. On one notorious occasion in 1790 a determined attempt was made to rig the election. Parson and White reported

> When during the progress of the election, the Corporation introduced into their books the names of no fewer than 1400 individuals, who they contended were thenceforth admitted to all the rights and privileges of freemen; and the candidates in the yellow interest [Tory], by means of this alleged majority, were returned.

The election result, however, was rescinded after the matter was taken to a Committee of the House of Commons, who decided that the new constituents, or mushrooms, as they were called, had no right to exercise the election franchise. Two members of the blue party (Whigs) were consequently elected.[8]

The franchise for the parliamentary elections, and for the municipal elections, were however radically changed by Acts of 1832 and 1835 respectively. The 1832 Reform Act enacted that the rights of voting in a Borough were to be enjoyed by every male person of full age in occupation as 'owner or tenant, any house, warehouse, counting house, shop of the clear yearly value of not less than ten pounds'.[9] A Freeman, or Burgess, resident in the Borough kept his right to vote if duly registered, according to the provisions of the Act, on the Rester of Voters, but this right was not extended to Freemen or Burgesses created since 1 March 1831 otherwise in respect of birth or servitude.[10]

The electorate post-1832 was strongly middle-class and property-owning. In the election of 1832 the Whigs gained a huge majority and subsequently there was a predominant, but not complete Whig dominance. While both Whig and Tory M.P.s were closely related to the large landowner class there was an increasing injection of industrialists to the Whig/Liberal ranks. John Dixon was returned as a Carlisle M.P. in 1847, Joseph Ferguson in 1852 and Joseph's son Robert in 1874, 1880 and 1885.

The Second Reform Act of 1867 gave the vote in the boroughs of all tenants and most lodgers with a residential qualification of at least 12 months thus drawing many working class citizens into the electorate. The total votes in the 1868 election in Carlisle was thereby increased to 230% of the previous total, with the Liberals remaining in control. Carlisle had the right to nominate 2 Members of Parliament for most of the 19th century but Carlisle seats were reduced to 1 in 1885 with Robert Ferguson retaining his seat.[11]

When the Municipal Corporation Act of 1835 became law[12] the old corporation was transformed into a new one which consisted of ten aldermen and thirty councillors and the corporate body was styled 'The Mayor, Aldermen and Burgesses of the City of Carlisle'. Under the authority of the Act the city was divided into five wards, the citizens or burgesses of each ward elected six councillors who retained their office for three years. The aldermen were appointed by the councillors for a period of six years, while the major was elected by the council.[13]

A councillor or alderman had to be a person of some substance as the Act specified that he should be in possession of real or personal estate to the value of £1,000 or more, or to be rated to the relief of the poor to an annual value of not less than £30. The electorate for the election of councillors were the burgesses who were defined 'as every male occupying any house, warehouse, counting house, or shop for three years, resident within seven miles, and paying rates for the relief of the poor.

The burgess, rather than the freeman, was now the privileged citizen. He had parliamentary and municipal voting rights, whereas the freeman, as such, only had a parliamentary vote. The freeman lost his exclusive right of trading but his rights of property and beneficial exemption were retained. The poor and under privileged were as before, with no voting rights at either the parliamentary, or municipal elections. They remained a discontented 'lower order' of society.

The legislation of the 1835 Act gave corporations considerable powers to provide services and amenities, without having to apply for special Acts of Parliament, but they were restricted in what they could do by the reluctance of the burgesses, the ratepayers, to foot the bill.

NOTES

1 The Charter is recorded in almost identical terms by many of the 18th and 19th century historians. I have quoted from J. Nicholson and R. Burn, *The History and Antiquities of the Counties of Westmorland and Cumberland* Vol. 2 (1777), pp. 240–2.

2 Ibid.

3 Parson and White, op. cit., p. 126.

4 M. Creighton, *Historic Towns – Carlisle* (1889), p. 193

5 Parson and White, op. cit., p. 126.

6 Ibid.

7 Ibid.

8 Parson and White, op. cit., p. 127.

9 2 Will IV c.45, *An Act to Amend the Representation of the People in England and Wales* (1832).

10 Ibid.

11 McCalmont, *Parliamentary Poll Book* (1971).

12 5 & 6 Will IV c.76, *An Act to provide for the Regulation of Municipal Corporations in England and Wales*.

13 Bulmer (1884), op. cit., p. 62.

Appendix 9

The Dixons – Cotton entrepreneurs

Peter Dixon (1753–1832) born Whitehaven, married Mary, daughter of Robert Ferguson in 1783. Leased Langthwaite cotton mill from Fergusons in 1807. Later lived at Tullie House.

Sons:

Peter John (1791–1866). he built a mansion at Holme Eden in 1837.
John (d. 1857). Built his mansion at Knells (Houghton) in 1826.
George (d. 1860). Blencogo and Tullie House. See portrait.

Grandsons:

John (b. 1829). Son of Peter John.
Peter James and Robert Sturdy. Sons of John (who died 1857). When the firm went bankrupt the two grandsons and related Joseph Forster were partners in the firm.

Shaddon Mills was built by Peter Dixon's sons in 1836 for the spinning of cotton. Initially weaving was carried out in outworkers' cottages, but in the 1840s the Dixons built a commodious building adjacent to their factory and installed several hundred power looms. Nevertheless weaver outworkers persisted until 1871 until they were entirely superseded by power loom operators. Dixons had a peak labour force of 8,000 of which 1,000 were employed in their factories.

In 1872 the firm went bankrupt with debts of £66,500.

REFERENCES

See my earlier chapters for more detail and to notes by D. R. Perriam on 'Peter Dixon & Sons and their factory buildings' in the County local history library.

Appendix 10

The Nuclear Power Industry in Cumbria

Calder Hall with finally, 4–60MW magnox reactors commissioned in 1956 was the first commercial nuclear power station in the world. The reactors with nuclear fuel, magnesium alloy encased, graphite moderated has carbon dioxide coolant which passed through a heat exchanger to supply steam to turbo-alternators. The reactors have proved extremely reliable with a load factor over a year of 85%.

British Nuclear Fuels, the production group of the U.K.A.E.A. operates the power station and provides services to fabricate the fuel rods, reprocess irradiated

On 17 October 1956 Her Majesty the Queen opened the world's first full-size atomic power station at Calder Hall. The Queen toured the station at 12 noon and pulled a switch that sent the first atomic-made electricity into the national grid.

rods, control the disposal of storage of radioactive material and decommissions redundant plant.

They provide service facilities for the following generation of Advance Gas Cooler reactors, fuelled by uranium and plutonium, and for the reprocessing of the fuel rods in the Thermal Oxide Reprocessing plant (Thorp).

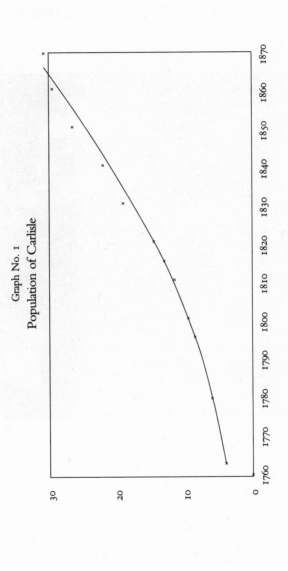

Graph No. 1
Population of Carlisle

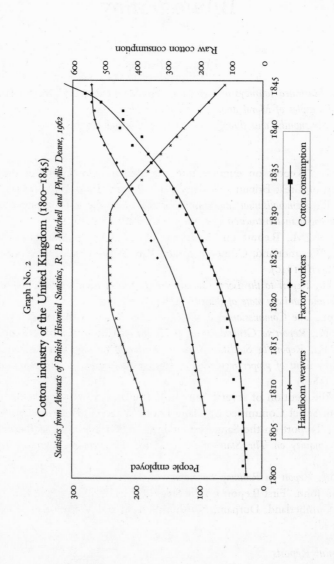

Graph No. 2

Cotton industry of the United Kingdom (1800–1845)

Statistics from Abstracts of British Historical Statistics, R. B. Mitchell and Phyllis Deane, 1962

Handloom weavers ✕   Factory workers ◆   Cotton consumption ■

Bibliography

Primary Sources

Fiennes, C., *Illustrated Journeys of Celia Fiennes 1682–1712*, ed. C. Morris (1982).
Paley, W., *Principles of Moral and Political Philosophy* (1785).
Young, A., *Six months tour through the north of England* (1770).

Reports

Chadwick, E., 'Report on enquiry into the Sanitary Conditions of the Labouring Population of Great Britain', *House of Lords Political Tracts P1172* (1842).

Chadwick, E., *Demoralisation and injuries occasioned by the want of proper regulations of labourers engaged in construction and working on Railways* (1845).

Muggeridge, R. M., Report on conditions of Hand Loom Weavers of counties of Lancaster, Westmorland, Cumberland and Part of West riding of Yorkshire, *Parliamentary Papers* (1840).

Power, W. H., *Report to the Local Government Board on recent epidemic prevalence of fever in Carlisle and sanitary state of the city* (1874).

Pringle, Capt., *The Commissioners of the Poor Laws Report, xviii* (1834).

Rawlinson, R., *Report to General Board of Health on City of Carlisle* (1850)

Rawlinson, R., *Report to Statistical Society of Manchester on Demoralisation and injuries occasioned by want of proper regulation of labourers engaged in construction and working of Railways.* (1847)

'Report on the Petition of several Weavers', *Parliamentary Papers* (1808).

'Report from Select Committee on Hand Loom Weavers', *Parliamentary Papers* (1835).

Reid, D. B., 'Report on the Sanitary Condition of Carlisle', *Second Report of Commissioners of Enquiry on The State of Large Towns and Populous Districts*, Appendix to part 2 (1845).

Select committee Report on Railway Labourers vol. 13 (1846).

Walsham, Sir John, 'First Report on the State of the Dwellings of the Labouring classes (no. 14), Cumberland, Durham, Northumberland and Westmorland', *Political Tracts P1173* (1840).

Carlisle Canal Reports

Chapman, W., *Report on the means of obtaining a safe and commodious communication from Carlisle to the sea* (1807).

Chapman, W., *Report of the Proposed Canal Navigation between Carlisle and the Solway Firth* (1818).

Chapman, W., *Report on the cost and separate advantage of ship canal or railway from Newcastle to Carlisle* (1824).

Directories and Gazetteers

Arthur's Guide to Carlisle (1881).

Bailey, J. and Culley, G., Generla view of Agriculture in Cumberland (1794).

Bulmer, T., History and Directory of East Cumberland (1884).

Carlisle Directory (1792).

Carlisle Directory (1837).

Guide to Carlisle (1821).

Hutchinson, W., History and Antiquities of Carlisle (1794).

Jefferson, S., History and Antiquities of Carlisle (1838).

Jollie's Directory (1811).

Lyson, Magna Britannia (1816).

Mannix and Whellan, History, Gazetteer, and Directory of Cumberland (1847).

Nicholson, J. and Burns, R., History and Antiquities of Counties of Westmorland and Cumberland vol. 2 (1777).

Nutter, M. E., Carlisle in Olden Times (1845).

Parson, W. and White, W., History, Directory and Gazetteer of Counties of Cumberland and Westmorland (1829).

Picture of Carlisle and Directory (1810).

Todd, H., Account of City and Diocese of Carlisle (1699).

Universal British Directory (1790).

Whellen, W., History of Cumberland and Westmorland (1860).

Secondary Sources

Baines, E., History of Cotton Manufactures in Great Britain (1835).

Bouch, C. M. C., Prelates and People of the Lake Counties (1848)

Bouch and Jones, Short economic and social history of Lake Counties.

Bunt, C. G. B. and Ross, E. A., Two Centuries of English Chintz (1750–1950) (1957).

Carlisle Corporation Officers, Local Government of the City and Borough of Carlisle 1158–1958 (1958).

Charlton, J., Carlisle Castle (1985).

Deane, P., The First Industrial Revolution (1965).

Dod., R. C., Electoral Facts (1832–53) (1853).

Farish, W., Notes on progress of Carlisle – an autobiography (1872).

Ferguson, R. S., Cumberland and Westmorland MPs (1660–1867) (1871).

— Diocesan History of Carlisle (1889).

— History of Cumberland (1890).

— and Nanson, W., Some municipal records of Carlisle (1887).

Gatrell, V. A. C., Lenman, B. and Parker. G. (eds), Crime and Law. Social History and Crime in Western Europe since 1500 (1980).

Glass, D. V., Development of Population Studies (1975).

Gosling, P. F., Carlisle – an Archaeological Survey of the Historic Town (1970).

Hadfield, C. and Briddle, G., Canals of N. W. England vol. 2.

Hay, D., Albion's Fatal Tree. Crime in Society in 18th-century England (1975).

McCalmont, Parliamentary Poll Book (1971).

Marshall, J. D. and Walton, J. K., *The Lake Counties from 1830* (1981).

Mitchell, W. R. and Joy, D., *Settle–Carlisle Railway* (1979).

Perriam, D. R., *Carlisle in Camera* 1 and 2 (1988).

Pevsner, N., *Buildings of England – Cumberland and Westmorland* (1967).

Smith, K., *Carlisle* (1970).

Ure, A., *The Philosophy of Manufacturers* (1835).

Willis, B., *Survey of Cathedrals: York, Durham, Carlisle, Chester* (1727).

Wilson, J. (ed.), *Victoria County History of Cumberland* vol. 2 (1905).

Articles and Theses

Barnes, H., 'Presidential Address', *British Medical Journal* (1896).

Barnes, J., 'Popular Protest and Radical Politics (1790–1850)', Ph.D. thesis, Lancaster (1981).

Dobson, R. B., 'Cathedral Chapters and Cathedral Cities, York, Durham and Carlisle in the 15th century', *N. H.* (1953).

Hopkinson, R., 'Elections in Cumberland and Westmorland (1695–1785)', Ph.D. thesis, Newcastle (1973).

Taylor, A., 'The Dukery of Carlisle', *Country Life* (1989).

Walton, J., 'Railways and Resort Development – Silloth', *N. H.* (1979).

Woodall, B. G., 'Carlisle Mails', *Philatelist* (1950).

Index